KAREN Y. BARNSTABLE

Seeking Silver

IN EVERY LIFE EXPERIENCE

Published by: Castle Quay Books
Burlington, ON, Canada | Riviera Beach, FL, USA
Tel: (416) 573-3249
E-mail: info@castlequaybooks.com | www.castlequaybooks.com

Cover design and book interior by Burst Impressions

Some names have been changed to protect the privacy of individuals.

Library and Archives Canada Cataloguing in Publication

Title: Seeking silver : in every life experience / by Karen Y. Barnstable.

Names: Barnstable, Karen Y., author.
Identifiers: Canadiana 20200162519 | ISBN 9781988928272 (softcover)

Subjects: LCSH: Barnstable, Karen Y. | LCSH: Christian biography. | LCSH: Christian women—
    Biography. | LCSH: Life change events—Religious aspects—Christianity. | LCGFT: Autobiographies.

Classification: LCC BR1725.B37 A3 2020 | DDC 270.092—dc23

CASTLE QUAY BOOKS

"Indeed, if you call out for insight and cry aloud for understanding,
and if you *look for it as silver* and search for it as hidden treasure,
then you will understand the fear of the Lord
and find the knowledge of God."
Proverbs 2:3–5, emphasis added

Contents

PROLOGUE

Smoke-filled skies blocked our view as we listened to the weather advisory for the Okanagan. Forest fires were raging. Air quality was so poor, we were advised to stay indoors. I paced around my house. My beach bag brimming with summer fun taunted me from the closet. Restless boredom threatened to take hold as I peered out at the gloomy red-tinted haze covering the valley.

What should I do? How should I make the most of being stuck in the house this summer? The idea came instantly. Write. Just write. Dig out old journals and get back to all of the unfinished pages. *What to write?* That was easy. Life experiences.

By the end of the summer, I had a collection of significant memories about my life captured on paper. But much more important than the first draft that had been created, I had had a revelation, a cathartic experience. Somehow, in the thinking and the writing about my life, I had renewed clarification of how my life all fit together. I had a glimpse of God's purpose and plan for me as I was being "knit together" (Psalm 139:13) in my mother's womb. I noticed, with a fresh perspective, how the silver threads of God had designed a purpose and plan for me. I could also see with clearer vision how God had been near to me in every life situation. He had responded to my every prayer, in a unique and personal way for each request, even though I often missed the answer at the time.

It is my hope that as you read my life stories you will be inspired and motivated to dig out a journal and begin writing your life stories too. I pray that as you write your stories you will see the silver threads of God in the design of your life and that His presence in your life experiences will be revealed.

If you are drawn to this invitation to begin writing, the following process may help you. After you read my stories, consider how they relate to situations or experiences in your life.

REFLECT.

Questions are included after every chapter to inspire your reflection and recall of your past experiences, thoughts, and emotions.

With all of these thoughts and reflections buzzing through your mind, start writing.

WRITE YOUR STORY.

Include everything that comes to your mind, even if it is painful. The mental and physical act of writing has the potential to bring healing and relief. It may enable you to reframe your experience and gain a new understanding of why all of these things happened to you.

Writing your stories may help you understand your life purpose and the unique plan that God has for your life. May you see your life from God's perspective and gain insight about life experiences that have puzzled you.

If the reflection and writing process leaves you with more questions and difficult memories to process, I encourage you to **shift your focus upward.**

PRAY.

Pray over the reflections that you have just experienced. Commit your thoughts and emotions to God and ask Him to show you His perspective of your life.

WRITE YOUR PRAYERS.

I encourage you to **write prayers** to God, asking Him your every unanswered question. Leave space in your journal below your prayers to return later and record answers that God has given you.

I am praying for you, dear reader, and have included a prayer after each reflection to help bring all of your experiences and thoughts to God. May He comfort you and give you His peace.

> **"And the peace of God, which transcends all understanding,**
> **will guard your hearts and your minds in Christ Jesus."**
> Philippians 4:7

THE FOUR DIMENSIONS OF REFLECTION

When we purposefully and meaningfully reflect on our experiences, we can deepen our learning and gain added perspective. The questions in this book are intended to guide you through purposeful reflection on your life experiences. They will lead you to four different perspectives, known as the four dimensions of reflection. The last chapter of this book explains how I created the four dimensions of reflection, which include thinking back, thinking inward, thinking outward, and thinking forward.

You can use the following guide to reflect on any significant event or season in your life when you learned by doing (i.e., walking through a cancer journey with a family member or friend) or a specific learning pursuit (i.e., attending a workshop or taking a course).

I. THINKING BACK

Reflecting on a learning experience or recalling a learning event after it has taken place enables you to revisit the experience from a fresh and different perspective. You may remember previously gained knowledge that was buried or forgotten.

Questions that help uncover learning from the past:
- What was the original purpose of this project/experience?
- What was your motive for completion of this project/experience?
- What were the critical factors helping or hindering completion of this project?
- What specific skills/knowledge/attributes were necessary for completion of this project?
- What did you learn from this project/experience?
- When did the most learning occur? How do you know this?

II. THINKING INWARD

Introspective reflections help us to engage our emotions. Reflecting on a previous experience is more meaningful when it connects to our emotions that we felt at the time. A deeper understanding of our own feelings and emotions leads to a higher level of learning.

Questions that lead to an intrinsic connection:
- Why was this project or experience meaningful to you?
- What are your personal beliefs regarding this learning experience?
- Do you agree or disagree with the way you learned this? Why or why not?
- What differences has the learning made in your intellectual, personal, or ethical development?
- What were the highest and lowest emotional moments in your learning experience?

III. THINKING OUTWARD

Reflecting on the world around us requires an extended point of view. Identifying the attitudes and opinions of another person, such as a family member, a friend, an author, a co-worker, or a person from another culture, leads us to further consideration of our own belief systems. The value in these contrasts and comparisons of beliefs is that it causes us to either expand our personal point of view or become more affirmed in our reasons for believing the way we do. Reflecting outwardly may lead to new ideas or perspectives on our experiences.

Questions that encourage extrinsic reflection:

- How are you looking at this topic? Can you identify another point of view?
- How might a person from another culture or religion look at this?
- Which of these viewpoints makes the most sense?
- Is your current concept about a topic causing problems for others?
- Does the problem or question in your mind have historical, ethical, scientific, political, or economic considerations?

IV. THINKING FORWARD

As we reflect on how we would do things differently in the future, we approach learning with added potential for insight. A deeper level of learning occurs with hindsight, along with gained wisdom and an enriched perspective.

Questions that lead to understanding future implications:

- If you had chosen to do "x" or not to do "x," what might have happened?
- How significant are the outcomes of either direction?
- If you had the chance to do this again, what changes would you make?
- How might this project or experience shape the goals that you set for your future?
- How might what you have learned affect your future learning decisions?

It is my hope that these four dimensions of reflection will add to your body of knowledge about your past experiences and increase your wisdom and understanding as you reflect, journal, and pray about your life story.

CHAPTER 1

Desperate

Every bone in my body trembled. Shivers from the tension and the cold pulsed through my veins. My coat was still inside. With my arms wrapped around my body, I crouched as low as I could go, hiding behind a car in the parking lot of a crowded nightclub. I tried to tell myself that he wouldn't be able to find me there. My eyes peered uselessly into the darkness, looking for a shadow I didn't want to see.

How did I end up in this terrifying place?

The car belonged to a classmate of mine from university who had given me a ride. She was still in the bar along with the other friends who had come with us.

How long will it take for them to come out? Am I safe here in the parking lot, or is this the most dangerous place to be? Will he find me here?

The heavy wooden door of the club creaked a threat every time it opened and closed. Footsteps crunched on the pavement. I tried to focus on my plan of action. I needed to think of a way to protect myself if he found me.

I prayed with desperation.

Lord, please protect me. Please keep me safe from him. I don't know why I came here, Lord. Please help me to get home safely.

The plans for the evening sounded like fun the day before. Two classmates from one of my university classes invited me to a party. I didn't know them outside of class but sat next to them in a mandatory course, bonding with them over our shared sense of humour. We kept ourselves engaged in the boring class by counting the mispronounced repetitions of our foreign professor with a thick accent. We created a code to decipher his poor pronunciations, rolled our eyes at each other, and snickered silently during the lectures.

When we chatted after class, I let it slip that my usual gang of friends had gone home for the weekend and I had no plans for Saturday evening. They convinced me to come to a "fun" party with them where many other classmates would be hanging out. They asked for my address and generously offered to give me a ride.

As soon as I got to the party Saturday evening, I realized I had made a fateful choice. The putrid smoky air reeked of marijuana, liquor, and drugs of every kind. I tried to stick close to my classmates, but it didn't take long for them to forget about me. They disappeared into the crowd diving into the alcohol and drugs that were available. I noticed some familiar faces from my classes and started awkward conversations with a few who seemed sober. Music blared, pounding the beat into our heads.

A few hours dragged by, and then the party was on the move. The gang of partyers decided they needed more room to dance, so they were heading to a popular nightclub.

If only I'd brought my own car.

My classmates ignored my plea for a ride back to my place and dragged me along to the bar. My excuses fell flat since they needed me to be their designated driver.

It was there, on the dance floor of the nightclub, where I found myself in an unexpected and terrifying trap. It started with an invitation that seemed innocent. A good-looking, strong, athletic guy came up to our table and insisted that I dance with him. I had no interest in this dancing partner, but he was not the type to take "no, thank you" for an answer. He kept insisting I dance with him, so I consented. Even though the first few dances were fairly harmless, something about my partner started to make me feel uncomfortable. I was grateful that the bar would close soon, and I could get out of there.

After several songs, the lights dimmed, and the music slowed down for a more intimate dance. I politely thanked my partner and tried to leave the dance floor. He grabbed my arm and yanked me back towards him. He squeezed his arms around me in a tight grip that wouldn't allow me to move. I struggled, but he pulled my body more tightly against his. He pressed his lips into my ear and spoke a claim on me that sent shivers of dread into my body and soul.

"You're mine tonight, bitch."

I danced the last slow dance in a frozen, rigid state, firmly stuck in the grip of my aggressive partner. I tried to get a glimpse of my classmates, but they were lost in the crowd of partyers, oblivious to the dangerous man holding me captive.

As the song came to a close and the other dancers began to separate, my dance partner lightened his grip slightly. With every ounce of fight that I could muster, I squirmed out of his grasp. I frantically scanned the club for my friends, but they were nowhere in sight. My eyes landed on the exit door, and I ran towards it as fast as my trembling legs would go. I fled for safety to the parking lot, hiding behind the wheel of my classmate's car. The keys were in her purse. I huddled there, hoping he hadn't seen which direction I went. I didn't look back. Had he followed me? If he found me now, I was an easy target. I was completely vulnerable in the parking lot, and no one would hear me if I screamed.

What a stupid move.

As I crouched next to the passenger door of my classmate's car, shivering with cold, fear, and embarrassment, I tried to think of how I could get help. Going back into the club was not an option.

Pray, just pray.

With my eyes wide open, still peering with dread into the darkness, I repeated the same prayer several times.

Lord, please protect me. Please keep me safe from him. Please help my friends to come out soon. I don't know why I came here, Lord. Please help me to get home safely.

As the minutes passed by, my terror lessened. I tried to tell myself that if he was still looking for me in the parking lot, he would have found me by now. I was freezing, but there was no way I was going back into that bar.

A distinct memory from a few weeks before invaded my thoughts. It was the last thing I wanted to think about at the time, but the reality of my situation brought back the vivid details of this recent frightful memory.

My roommate and I were sound asleep in our apartment, the window propped open for fresh, cool air. We were both startled at two in the morning by a terrifying scream that pierced the night. It came from one of the parking lots eight storeys below our apartment in the student residences. We told ourselves it was probably just some kids partying and goofing around and went back to sleep. We heard the next morning that a female student had been the victim of a rape in the area of our residence. It had happened in a parking lot.

Rumours surrounding the rape were all over campus, and I wasn't sure about the full truth behind the stories, but there was no doubt that the girl who was attacked that night was devastated. She quit university and moved back home. Her rapist had not been identified or caught. He was still at large.

It seemed like hours before my classmates came out of the club and found me, still crouching by the wheel of the car. I tried to tell them about my fearful situation, but they were too inebriated to care. They just laughed it off. I was the designated driver, once again, despite my trembling hands. I manoeuvred my classmate's car mechanically down one street, one corner at a time, ignoring the ridiculous jabber of my intoxicated crew. I'm still not sure how we all managed to get home safely that night, but we did.

Was it just luck, or had God answered my feeble, desperate prayer?

As I lay safe and sound in bed at the student residence, I realized that I had survived a threatening situation that could have turned out like the girl who had been raped in the parking lot just below my residence. God protected me and spared me from a potentially life-devastating situation.

YOUR STORY:

A Place of Fear

THINKING BACK

- Have you ever been in a life-threatening position or a place of total fear where you knew something devastating could happen to you? Where were you at the time, and what were you doing at that location?
- What personal thoughts or choices led you to finding yourself in this position?

THINKING INWARD

- How did your body respond, physically and mentally, to the fearful situation?
- What was your greatest fear about what could happen or what the end result of this situation might be?

THINKING OUTWARD

- Who else was involved? Was there anyone who could have or should have come to your rescue?
- It is a natural response to "hide" memories of fear in our memory vault. Have you shared your memory of fear with someone you trust? Did you sense God's presence with you at the time?

THINKING FORWARD

- What have you learned from your past fearful experience(s) to guide you in the future?
- What area of your life still brings you fear or is in need of God's protection today?

Write a Prayer: Share all of your fears with God and ask Him to protect you from harm and help you conquer the fears.

Dear Heavenly Father,

Your word says that You are an ever-present help in times of trouble (Psalm 46:1) and that You are a refuge and a shield (Psalm 119:114), protecting us in ways we cannot see. I pray that You would protect us and show us how You are helping us through life's hardships and fearful situations. Remove fear from our lives today, and help us to trust in You.

In Your name, amen.

"God is our refuge and strength,
an ever-present help in trouble."

PSALM 46:1

CHAPTER 2
Confused

I read and reread the university programs with longing. There were so many appealing options, I wanted to sign up for every one of them.

Typical me. Interested in everything but not naturally gifted in anything.

Not one single gold ribbon existed in my keepsake box, but I had participation ribbons of every kind. I won an athletic award in high school for participating in every intramural sport that was offered. I caught a ride with the neighbours to attend the awards ceremony and receive my award. My parents didn't come.

Most of my friends in high school were not only encouraged by their parents, they were expected to attend university. But that was not the case with my family. A good job that taught work ethics and allowed you to save some money was the goal to pursue.

Neither of my parents had attended university. My mom had not even had the chance to graduate from high school. My dad, a self-made successful man through hard work and good business choices, had become financially secure without an education. He thought that university would be a waste of time and money for his second oldest daughter, convinced that I would get married and start a family and that the money spent on that education would be wasted.

The private discussions my parents had about important matters were held in their first language, German. My sisters and I did not learn any German. It seemed that German was a "secret language" our parents used when they didn't want us to know what they were saying. I wondered what they actually said to each other about my career ambitions.

Even though university education was not encouraged, my parents insisted that each one of their four daughters attend one year of Bible college. We could choose the college that we wanted to attend as long as we completed one year of general Bible studies. There were college options a few hours away from where we lived, but my sense of adventure and desire for independence led me to choose a college two provinces away from our home in Saskatchewan.

I picked a college in Peterborough, Ontario. The reason my parents allowed this was because my mom's sister lived in Peterborough. My aunt had been an elementary teacher in the Peterborough School District. Her missionary friend and roommate taught at the college. One of my favourite courses at the college was the course my aunt's friend instructed on Christian education. I sang in the college ensemble that travelled most weekends, singing in churches all around Ontario and Quebec. The weekend that I loved above all others was the weekend I was billeted with a French-speaking family. I used my high school French to the peak of my learnings but craved to communicate better with them.

French had been my favourite subject and my highest mark all through high school. My French teacher told us a few stories about his sideline work as a translator for the provincial courts in our city. Those stories made a huge impression on me. The naive career dream of becoming a translator formed in my mind.

The next fall, I enrolled at the University of Saskatchewan in Saskatoon, despite my parents' opinions. I was going to major in linguistics and continue taking French classes but also study German and Spanish at the same time. I had lofty dreams of knowing many languages and becoming a translator.

My first year of university was fraught with frustrations and disappointments. My linguistics class was a snoozefest, boring me to tears. Any future classes in this career field would involve the same professor. My French marks were excellent, but all other marks were barely average. Just before reading week, I hit an all-time low. My studies seemed pointless and my career track impossible.

What was I thinking? A translator!? What a ridiculous career plan. I should have listened to my parents. They were right.

I thought about packing it in and going home to find a job like my dad had wanted me to do from the start. I decided to pray about what I should do with my life.

Dear Lord, Your word says that You have a plan for our lives. You said in Jeremiah 29:11, You have "plans to prosper you and not to harm you, plans to give you hope and a future." But I don't feel much hope right now, Lord. You know that I love French and just want to keep learning it. I thought a translator job would be cool, Lord, but I can see that it's not going to work for me. I don't want to quit and go home, but I can't keep taking classes for nothing and I'm running out of money. What should I do, Lord? Please give me some career direction. Amen.

The career path of a teacher was not my first choice at the time, but by accident I discovered that if I transferred to the faculty of education with a French major, I would be eligible for a scholarship of two thousand dollars each year of my studies. I could continue studying French, and my dad would be relieved about the financial help I would be getting. This was a win-win, an obvious decision.

The next three years of studies in education were more satisfying than I expected. I engaged wholeheartedly in all of my classes, especially my French methodology class. My prof for this course was a delight, demonstrating useful instructional methods for our future teaching in the most fun-loving, enthusiastic manner. She was a true role model. My practicum experiences were stressful, but I received many positive affirmations about my ability to teach. My supervising teacher in Radisson Secondary School drafted a complimentary report about me that I value today, especially since he said that my French was that of a "frog," a native French speaker.

I was content to the core at my convocation, accepting proof of my bachelor of education with a major in French and a minor in English.

The most rewarding part of the convocation, however, was that my mom and my dad decided to attend. My dad was so proud of me, he got emotional. I couldn't recall ever seeing my dad cry before. This unexpected reaction from him made me realize the significance of my accomplishment. I was the first in our family to receive a university degree.

Was it God who led me to finding out about the scholarship for French teachers?

I believe that God answered my simple prayer for career guidance. He knew, so much better than I did, just how well-suited I was for a career as an educator. I have heard the testimonies of others who have experienced divine guidance to their profession. It looked like I had received heavenly nudges towards a career choice that was perfectly suited for me.

YOUR STORY:

Goals and Ambitions

THINKING BACK
- What were the career goals and ambitions that you had in your early life?
- Who or what created an impression on you to develop those ambitions?

THINKING INWARD
- What aspect of your career has been the most satisfying or fulfilling for you? Can you recall a peak moment of satisfaction and identify why it was a highlight?
- What has been the most challenging or frustrating? Can you identify the cause of the frustration?

THINKING OUTWARD
- Were there specific people or events that influenced your career goals, causing you to see them differently?
- Has a co-worker or boss commented on your work skills or abilities in a positive or negative way, creating a lasting impression on you?

THINKING FORWARD
- What aspects of your career(s) are you the most grateful for today? Have you acquired skills or abilities that you can use in your future?
- Do you have goals, dreams, or ambitions that you are seeking for your future?

Write a Prayer: Commit your career questions and desires to God and ask for His guidance today.

Dear Heavenly Father,

You know us so well. You created us with unique talents and abilities that line up with Your purposes for our lives. You are fully aware of people in our lives who have helped or hindered us from experiencing clear direction or satisfaction in our careers. I lift up those words from people in our lives to You, Lord, and ask You to guide us to the truth. Help us to see Your perspective on our lives. Continue leading us, Lord, through our goals and dreams, and direct us to the next thing You have planned for us to do.

In Your name, amen.

"Many are the plans in a person's heart, but it is the LORD's purpose that prevails."

PROVERBS 19:21

CHAPTER 3

Smitten

I had no idea that this ordinary Sunday would turn out to be a life-altering day. I was sitting in the back row of a large church next to a whole row of young men I had never met. My friend from choir had led me to this seat, then left abruptly. I sat there alone, feeling awkward and out of place. The guy sitting next to me was equally uncomfortable, shifting his feet back and forth nervously. It was hard to ignore his restless feet since they were huge, size 12 or larger, I thought, and were not at all minimized in tan-coloured boots with rounded toes and chunk heels.

What is this guy's problem? His tension is making mine worse.

It wasn't the church service that was making me feel out of place. I had attended there regularly for the last two years, ever since I started my studies at the University of Saskatchewan. I had joined the choir and sang in an ensemble that was featured on the church's televised program on Sunday afternoons. The choir usually only sang on Sunday mornings, but this was Sunday evening, and we had been asked to sing for a very unique and unusual service about relationships. It was a program designed for youth, especially college- and career-aged people.

After the choir finished singing, we were instructed to go to the back of the auditorium and find a place to sit. The dynamic speaker had a special message about sex in relationships. At the end of his talk, he asked all of the young men who wanted to live for God and be an example in their relationships to stand up. The guy with the big feet stood, along with a hundred other young men in the auditorium. He shifted even more nervously from foot to foot as he stood. Then the speaker asked all the young women who wanted to live for God and be a support to these young men to now stand up. I felt a tug in my heart leading me to stand. While on our feet, the young women were instructed to pray for these young men to be positive examples in their relationships.

Not knowing how to pray for a hundred guys I did not know, I decided to pray for Mr. Big Foot next to me. I prayed in earnest for the young man I had not yet met, with no idea as to why I was praying for him in particular.

Dear Lord, please be very near to this guy next to me who seems so nervous. Help him to honour You in all he does. Protect him in his relationships and help him to resist sexual temptations that come his way. Guide and direct him in his life choices and help him to be the man of God he desires to be. Amen.

When the service came to a close we were all invited to go for coffee and snacks in the church gym. To my relief, my friend from choir showed up again and introduced me to the stranger who sat next to me. It was her brother Kim, who had recently moved to the city for work. My friend had told me about this brother she thought I should meet, but I hadn't paid much attention.

I couldn't actually get a good look at her brother during the introduction since his gaze turned downward as we were introduced. Awkward words and phrases bounced back and forth. Our conversation wasn't going anywhere, so I decided to make a quick exit. I explained that I had an exam the next day I needed to study for, excused myself, and headed for the door.

Two nights later, the phone rang for me, twice. The first call was our choir director. Rehearsal was cancelled that night as she was not feeling well. I had an unexpected free night. Before I even had a chance to think about it, the phone rang again. It was my friend's brother, Kim. He sounded a lot more confident on the phone. He said he knew I had a free night since choir was cancelled and asked if I would like to go to a movie with him. Without an available excuse, I decided to accept his offer. I was thinking that a movie date would be fairly harmless. Not a lot of conversation would be needed. Besides, I had already prayed a pretty serious prayer for this guy. Maybe there was a reason.

An hour later, my door buzzer rang. As I opened the door, I was most pleasantly surprised. Kim looked directly at me, and I finally got a good look at him.

Whoa! Is this the same guy I met on Sunday? So glad I said yes to this date.

I wondered why I hadn't noticed how good-looking this guy was two nights ago. Not only was my date in fine form, he was also more relaxed than I expected, and our evening was off to a promising start.

I didn't return home until eight hours later. We walked all around campus by the university theatre while waiting for a later show, then realized that the show on campus was cancelled. We talked and talked as we walked. We found a movie at another theatre in town, then went for pizza after the show. Kim showed me the house where he lived with a few other guys. We sat by the pool in the backyard, continuing the easy flow of our ongoing conversation. We talked until two a.m. Throughout the evening we shared many stories about our lives. We told each other about our families, our past, our present, and our goals for the future. We had countless things in common. By the end of the night I was completely smitten.

When I finally got home, I told my roommate I was going to marry this perfect guy. Being more level-headed than I was at the time, she reasoned that he must have at least one flaw. I had to admit that he did, in fact, have one major flaw. He had a very unusual last name, a name that made no sense at all. My roommate and I had a good laugh as I told her that my perfect date's last name was Barnstable.

Before I drifted off to a peaceful sleep that dreamy night, I remembered a serious prayer I had prayed not long before, after the terrifying experience in a nightclub. I had asked God to help me find good friends and end my two-sided lifestyle. I knew I needed friends who believed in God and wanted to live their lives for Him. I reminded God about this prayer and thanked Him for the new friend I had just found.

Since my first date with Kim went so well, we planned the second date for two nights later. It was the Thursday before Thanksgiving, and we both wanted to see each other again before we travelled home to see our families for the long weekend. Kim picked me up with plans to treat me to an expensive dinner in a high-end restaurant. The upscale dining room was perched on the top floor of a five-star hotel. Our gourmet meals were presented in sophisticated style, but the fine cuisine and luxurious surroundings went unnoticed. Our gaze was fixed on each other as we sat across the table in a dreamlike daze of infatuation.

I could tell he wanted to kiss me, and the feeling was mutual. We couldn't wait till we reached the car. Our first kiss happened in the elevator as soon as we left the restaurant.

This date was much shorter than our first date since we both had commitments the next day. But as we said good night we both admitted that we could hardly wait for the long weekend to be over so we could see each other again.

Our conversation that evening revealed another layer of my handsome date. Besides our shared goals and beliefs, I discovered another trait that I respected and admired. Kim held tightly to his Christian standards. He had not compromised his faith and his values despite the many temptations of his sports world and the influences of his teammates.

Could it be that he is the answer to my prayers?

YOUR STORY:

Infatuation and Love

THINKING BACK

- Who was the first person that you fell in love with? What attracted you to this person initially?
- What circumstances led to your first encounter with each other?

THINKING INWARD

- What feelings or emotions did you experience as you got to know this special person?
- What aspects of their personality did you admire the most? What made these traits appealing to you?

THINKING OUTWARD

- Before you met each other, did you have an idea in mind of the type of person you were hoping to find? Did anyone or any couples influence your view of a desired relationship?
- Did family members or friends comment on your relationship or your compatibility?

THINKING FORWARD

- What have you learned from your past romantic relationship(s) that influences the person you are today and how you view the future?
- What are the hopes and dreams you have for your relationship(s) of the future?

Write a Prayer: Tell God your thoughts and questions about the relationships in your life. Commit your heart's desire to Him.

Dear Heavenly Father,

You created us with the desire to be loved. Many of us enjoy watching a story of romance where two people who were meant to be together find each other. I pray Your blessing on the relationship desires of my readers, Lord, and ask that You would protect and guide each union that exists. And, dear Lord, You are aware of readers who have not experienced true love or have lost the one whom they love. I pray that You would comfort them, as only You can, and fill the void in their lives with Your love.

In Your name, amen.

"And so we know and rely on the love God has for us. God is love. Whoever lives in love lives in God, and God in them."

1 JOHN 4:16

CHAPTER 4

Accused

It was a crucial time in our relationship. Kim and I had been seeing each other for seven months, and we both wanted to see if our romance was going to move forward. We reached a fork in the road as my third year of university ended and decisions about how we would spend our summer had to be made.

Kim's location for the summer was already determined. He needed to return home to southeast Saskatchewan and help plant the crop on the family grain farm. His career plan as a farmer was already in place. I only had one year of education studies left, and then I could begin my career as a teacher. I had worked in Saskatoon the previous summer and knew that jobs would be available to me in my university city, but staying in Saskatoon for the summer meant Kim and I would be a five-hour drive from each other.

Should I stay here, or should I chance it in southeast Saskatchewan? If I can find a job there, we could have a romantic summer together.

It was a difficult choice, but with my heart leading my head, I began the search for a summer job in the town near Kim's family farm.

My resumé was impressive, listing the many jobs I had tackled since the age of 15. I had a continuous record of employment, often working more than one part-time job at a time. My experiences ranged from ice cream shops to high-end restaurants, shoe stores to clothing outlets, small business offices to government agencies. Two previous summer jobs had been spent as a clerk at Saskatchewan Government Insurance. That was the job my dad wanted me to keep long-term.

Estevan was a small city, but I remained hopeful I'd be able to find a job there. The options were few, but one posting for a teller at a local bank caught my eye right away. It wasn't advertised as a summer job, but the idea of this position appealed to me. Even though I had nothing like this work on my resumé, I applied for the position and managed to get an interview. I was hired immediately.

I passed the on-the-job training in record speed. Learning how to handle all types of bank transactions seemed straightforward and easy to master. I relished the chance to be a fully qualified teller, open my own station, and greet the customers.

As tellers, we were not allowed to open our individual stations until we had balanced all transactions from the day before. It took me a bit longer than the other tellers to balance, but I was usually up and running with my station soon after the experienced tellers.

One morning, a few weeks after I completed my training, I couldn't get my transactions to balance. I went over the statements repeatedly, but something was causing an error. My station remained closed as my supervisor scoured my transactions. No errors could be found. In total frustration, she finally let me open my station to keep up with the customers of the day despite the incomplete balancing requirement.

The same problem happened the next day. And the day after, it happened again, and again. Day after day, I could not balance. Each time, my supervisor had to set aside the demands of her regular work to comb through all my statements, trying to find an error. She couldn't find one. Her frustration with me turned to anger. She blamed me and accused me of hiding something. I was baffled by her accusations.

Why does this keep happening? Why can't I balance? I'm doing everything just as I was trained to do. In all the jobs I've worked, I've never caused anyone to be so angry.

The problem kept happening. I could not figure out how to balance. In exasperation, my supervisor discussed the issue with the bank manager. She filed a report about me that contained the only theory they could muster as to why I couldn't balance. From their perspective, I was stealing from the bank. My inability to balance each day indicated small amounts of missing funds. I would have to be watched with "high alert" to avoid further theft.

The report drafted about me was devastating. It was kept on file and had the potential to scar my employment record permanently.

The last thing I wanted Kim to hear about me was that I was deceitful or distrustful. I had moved to his corner of the province for the summer so that we could continue getting to know each other and our relationship could blossom. This job was not working in my favour.

How will I tell him about these work issues and this disastrous report? Does he know me well enough to realize these accusations are not true?

To my relief at the time, Kim was distracted and didn't realize the seriousness of my job trauma. Besides the long hours of farm work, he played fastball in a competitive league. A travelling baseball performance team arrived in Estevan and was practising with Kim's team for a high-action public performance. Kim was the star pitcher and was drawing a lot of attention from the team.

One of the team members was an attractive, athletic female player, a few years older than Kim and me. She swooned over my athletic boyfriend, causing him to blush and fidget nervously. I was not impressed with her forwardness around him and even less impressed by his reaction to her. Kim was so preoccupied with all this admiration, he wasn't even noticing me. My confidence in our relationship dipped to a disheartening low.

This was turning out to be the worst summer of my life. My work world was destroying my belief in myself to do a job well. On top of that, I was questioning everything about my relationship with Kim. My hopes and dreams for our future were eroding daily. I needed to pray.

Dear Lord, You know all about the predicaments I'm in this summer. You know how much I care about Kim and how worried I am about our relationship right now. You also know about the horrible accusations that have been written about me at the bank. I don't even know how to defend myself, Lord. I read verses today that say You will fight for us (Deuteronomy 20:4) and deliver us from our troubles (Psalm 34:19). I ask for this help today, Lord. Please guide me at the bank and help them to see that I'm not a thief. And, please protect Kim and me. Help him to see past the advances of the female baseball star. I was so sure when we met that we were meant for each other. I pray that this summer will not be wasted and that we could still move forward. In Your name I ask this, Lord. Amen.

The big weekend of the baseball performance show finally arrived. I was bursting with pride as my boyfriend demonstrated his pitching abilities for the crowd. The show was a huge success, with the fans "oohing" and "aahing" at the skills of the high-performance team. A barbecue was planned to celebrate the event after the show. I tried to enjoy the festivities, but I could hardly wait for the weekend to be finished. The travelling team would leave our town and move on to the next one. I would have time with Kim again and could find out if his heart was still mine.

The following week at the bank, an unexpected discovery was made about my errors. I often displaced two numbers that were close. Instead of typing $93.48, I would enter the numbers $93.84. These mistakes were subtle errors that were hard to find. This type of number mix-up happened often in my daily life with phone numbers or other numbers I was trying to remember. I just laughed it off. At the bank, a number error like that was no laughing matter.

Fortunately, recognizing my number displacements helped to identify and prevent errors. Balancing the transactions of the previous day was no longer an issue. I managed to complete my summer of working at the bank without further accusations.

On my last day of work, the bank manager called me into his office. I wasn't sure what to expect. He smiled and commented that it had been an interesting summer. He apologized for the harsh report that had been written about me. Now that the staff knew me better, they realized that the accusations were ludicrous. Right there, in front of me, he shredded the report. He knew I was planning a career as a teacher, and he had an important recommendation for me. We both laughed out loud as he suggested that I stick to teaching languages and avoid the subject of mathematics. I nodded in full agreement. I always knew I was better with words than numbers. That summer provided unforgettable evidence.

What a crazy summer! I am so relieved, but why did this all happen?

The end of that summer provided more evidence to continue believing in my relationship with Kim. The distractions of the female baseball star disappeared as smoothly as the shredded report. Kim and I had time with each other again and were soon back on track.

As the negative emotions of that summer dissolved and we talked more about our future, I was grateful to leave the bank job in good standing with all of the staff. If I came back to this town and worked as a teacher, it was possible that the children of the staff at that bank might be students in my future classrooms.

YOUR STORY:

Seeking Justice

THINKING BACK

- Have you ever been mistreated in some way or accused of something you did not do? How did the accusations come about?
- Did the accusations threaten your reputation? What type of damage did they cause?

THINKING INWARD

- How did the accusations affect your belief in yourself or confidence in your abilities?
- How did you cope with the inner turmoil of the situation?

THINKING OUTWARD

- Did the accusations change how you were viewed by others?
- Were you able to defend yourself? Was there anyone who did believe in you who could have defended you?

THINKING FORWARD

- What have you learned from past injustices that could guide you in dealing with them in your future?
- Are you experiencing the threat of false accusations today that may impact your future?

Write a Prayer: Tell God about any past or present mistreatment or accusations in your life. Ask Him to come to your defence.

Dear Heavenly Father,

You are already aware, dear Lord, that false accusations happen in many people's lives, destroying their reputation and their belief in themselves. I pray for every reader who has experienced and still is experiencing the deep trauma of this attack. Your word describes the agony of these accusations in Psalm 109 and says that You come to rescue us. It says that God "stands at the right hand of the needy, to save their lives from those who would condemn them" (Psalm 109:31). Help us, I pray, and rescue us from wrongs done to us.

In Your name, amen.

"You came near when I called you, and you said, 'Do not fear.' You, Lord, took up my case; you redeemed my life. LORD, you have seen the wrong done to me. Uphold my cause!"

LAMENTATIONS 3:57–59

CHAPTER 5

Questioning

I lingered over my second cup of coffee, gazing at the sparkling set of rings on my finger. Life had slowed down to a relaxing crawl after a whirlwind of events the past two months.

It started with my convocation from university, followed by a few short weeks of planning for our wedding day, topped off with our two-week honeymoon in Florida. Three incredible photo albums of beautiful memories were already behind me. I tried to focus on the perfect images from the amazing days of the last two months and ignore the familiar cloud of uncertainty that was threatening to rob me of my current state of joy.

Despite the joy and excitement of our engagement, the months leading up to our wedding brought some unexpected concerns. Kim was still living on the farm in southeast Saskatchewan, and I was back in Saskatoon, so we had to endure the five-hour distance between us from Christmas till June. Our demanding lives in opposite corners of the province lacked connection. Kim was back working on the farm, and I was finishing my practicum for teaching in Radisson, north of Saskatoon. Our communication via distance seemed empty of emotion. We met a few times to attend our premarital counselling, but the sessions were frustrating. Rather than help us understand each other better, they put more strain on our relationship. I began to question how well I really knew this guy who had captured my heart and if we were well-suited for each other or not. I began to pray in a different way for my future husband.

Dear Lord, You know my thoughts and fears about the man I am about to marry and the new life I will be starting with him. I thought I knew him, but some days, Lord, I am not sure. And does he really know me? Are we going to be good for each other? Will I be content living on a farm in south Saskatchewan? I have so many questions, Lord, and so I pray that if we are not meant for each other You would stop or block our plans. If this is truly meant to be, please calm my worries and guide our possible future together in every way. Thank You, Lord. Amen.

The day of our wedding was a rare day of perfect weather in Swift Current, Saskatchewan—sunny with no wind. There wasn't a single cloud in the sky. My oldest sister helped me with all of the planning details for the wedding. With her tasteful guidance, our colours of lilac infused with yellow accents were chosen. My bouquet of purple orchids with yellow roses was a standout feature that went well above the budget—nearly giving my dad a heart attack when he saw the bill a few weeks later.

The ceremony and the reception took place without a hitch, all according to plan, until an unexpected interruption near the end of the evening. The reception ended abruptly with a crazy attempt by Kim's cousins to steal the bride, an outdated tradition that lingered among Kim's family and friends. A ridiculous high-speed car chase took place like a scene out of a bad movie. The groom fled at full speed, his new bride at his side, with the cousins right behind in hot pursuit. Fortunately, no one was injured, and the only traces of the incident later were some car tracks on lawns and a dent in the bumper of my dad's Lincoln. My groom and I ended up safely back at the Horseshoe Hotel banquet room in time to express appreciation and farewell to our guests.

Much more important than the exquisite flowers or crazy car chases on our wedding day was my state of mind that perfect June day. The cloud of uncertainty that formed in my mind during our engagement was nowhere in sight. Not a single doubt or worry existed in my mind as we said our vows to each other on June 19, 1982.

Our two weeks in Florida floated by like blissful scenes on a honeymoon brochure coming to life. We toured around in our rented convertible, soaked up sun on the beach, revelled in the sights of Busch Gardens, and laughed at the kissing seals performing at Sea World.

When we returned to southeast Saskatchewan, we had a home waiting for us. Kim had rented a house trailer and moved it onto an empty lot in the town of Macoun, 20 minutes from Estevan. It arrived in a filthy mess, but my mother-in-law and my sister-in-law lovingly scrubbed it clean and moved our wedding gifts inside. It was a comfortable home, but only temporary, as Kim had already started building us a new home on an acreage a few miles outside of Macoun.

The fun and spontaneity of our honeymoon life faded quickly as we settled into the reality of our new lives in rural Saskatchewan. That was when the familiar cloud of concern rolled back in. Even though we lived under the same roof, our days were consumed with our individual work lives. Kim worked long hours on the farm and whenever possible worked on the building of our new house. By September, I was completely consumed with the demands of my first teaching job, so I left all of the decisions about the house with Kim. I felt guilty about not helping more with house decisions, but staying on top of daily teaching lessons plus coaching volleyball left little time or head space for house details. All I could do was pray for Kim and hope that God would give him wisdom to make good choices.

We had only been married six months when we moved into our brand new two thousand square foot ranch-style home on our acreage in a bare field. Our windows peered out to nothing but dirt and a water well. The inside was just as sparse since we barely had enough furniture for one of the rooms.

It didn't take long to move our few belongings into our new home. Life in the trailer had been cozy and close. I wondered if life would be as good in the new spacious home outside of town. When I got home from school, I wandered aimlessly from one freshly painted room to the next, trying to bask in the luxury of this huge blessing.

It's so big and beautiful, but it's empty and cold. Not a neighbour in sight. How will we stay close to each other in this house?

The threat of losing desired closeness with my new husband loomed in my mind as I tried to adjust to our new home in the country. I attempted to push all of the clouds of uncertainty away with prayer.

Dear Lord, I pray for Your blessing over our new home out in the country, in the bare field. Even though it is brand new and huge, it seems kind of empty and lonely. I pray that it will start to feel like a home, not just a house, as we get more settled. Lord, You know that I am just barely keeping my head above water with my teaching job, and I feel bad about not helping more with the house details. I thank You, Lord, for all of the knowledge about houses You have given to Kim and for all of the good decisions he has made. I also thank You for all of the help we have received from family to build and finish it. I pray that You would be honoured in our marriage and in our lives in this new house. Continue to bless us as a team of husband and wife in our new home, I pray. Amen.

Once again, my worries were in vain as life on the acreage became satisfying in a different way. We invested in new furniture, one piece at a time. We planted grass and hundreds of trees, and our farmyard began to take shape. With both of us making a good income we had no financial concerns. We made large payments on our mortgage and planned to have the home paid for in five years. It felt like we were getting established and would live there forever.

We're getting there, God. We're starting to find strength as a couple.

Little did we know that there would be many more homes, in many different places, and many more clouds in our future lives together. Change would come in the most unexpected ways, and our barely adjusted marriage in our new home in the country would be challenged to the core.

YOUR STORY:

Uncertainty

THINKING BACK

- How did your first experience of living with a partner come about?
- How did you find or choose your first home with your partner?

THINKING INWARD

- Did you have any worries or fears about what life would be like as you started living together?
- How were decisions about life choices made now that you were living as partners? Did you feel a sense of peace in your first home together?

THINKING OUTWARD

- Did your relationships with family members or friends change as your living situation changed? Did they provide any support for you?
- Did life expenses or joined finances transition smoothly or create conflict? Did you receive any guidance around joint finances?

THINKING FORWARD

- As you look around your home today, does it reflect influences of the past, or is your home an indication of future goals and plans?
- What is your greatest hope for your living situation in the future?

Write a Prayer: Commit your concerns and your desires for your living situation to God and ask Him for His blessing in your home.

Dear Heavenly Father,

You know the intimate thoughts, concerns, and regrets of every reader. You see and understand the sadness or pain that may be there due to complex issues of relationships and living situations. I pray, dear Lord, that You would comfort and heal all sorrow or wounds that this reflection may bring up. I pray over the homes that they live in, and I ask for Your peace and Your presence to prevail. As we envision our next home, we pray that every room will be "filled with rare and beautiful treasures" of knowledge that comes from You.

In Your name, amen.

"By wisdom a house is built,
and through understanding it is established;
through knowledge its rooms are filled
with rare and beautiful treasures."

PROVERBS 24:3–4

CHAPTER 6
Overwhelmed

I stared in awe at the tiny pointy-headed creature that had been placed in my arms. The birth, long and severely painful, left me doubting if my body would ever function normally again. All those books I read had not prepared me for this experience.

No one told me it would feel like this. Maybe I should have waited longer, or maybe I would never have been ready.

It was our plan from the beginning to wait five years before we started a family, and we stuck to the plan. Five busy but fulfilling years passed by like a movie scene in fast-forward. Kim was working long hours farming and playing competitive fastball most weekends. I was enjoying my teaching career and my contract work with the Saskatchewan Ministry of Education, writing curriculum and training new French teachers. We weren't at all sure that we were ready, but soon after our fifth anniversary, I became pregnant.

The pregnancy passed without sickness or any other issues. I was blessed with good health the full nine months despite being very tired with the demands of full-time teaching. I didn't have a lot of time to think about the huge change coming to our lives, which was probably for the best.

On May 23, 1987, our son Kolby Corray was born. His first name was the favourite of all the names we considered that started with "K." His middle name was a combination of the names Cornie, from my dad, and Ray, from Kim's dad. Despite the challenging circumstances around Kolby's birth, I will never forget the feeling of euphoria that I had as I first held my son.

During the pregnancy, I secretly hoped that my first child would be a boy. Kolby was a wish come true. He was a strong, masculine little dude from day one. His head was pointy for a few days due to the stress of the birth, but shortly thereafter a normal rounded shape returned. His body measured longer than most babies, with long legs to match. His feet were oversized for his little body, resembling his father right from the start.

My mom came from Swift Current to help me with the baby the first week. I was also blessed to have my sister-in-law and my mother-in-law close by if more help was needed. Breastfeeding felt natural, without complications, and Kolby grew at a healthy, normal pace. The routines of feeding, bathing, and sleeping created the rhythms of each day. My helpers went home, and soon I was left to handle things on my own. It seemed that everyone had returned to the normal pace of life when the reality of my new daily routine came crashing in on me.

For no apparent reason, Kolby started to cry every afternoon. Nothing I tried would settle him down. I rocked him, I walked him, I tried to nurse him again and again, but all he did was wail and wail. It was driving me crazy. I wanted to get in my car and drive away. I missed my teaching days, my teacher friends, and my students. I missed getting up in the morning well rested. I missed putting on professional clothes and heading out on the highway in my cute little car. I felt trapped. But the worst feeling of all was that I felt so guilty for having all of these thoughts.

What is wrong with me? Why can't I enjoy the blessings of motherhood?

I loved this little creature with all my heart, but he was really cramping my style. In a bundle of mixed emotions and tears, I turned to prayer.

Dear Lord, I am a mess. This baby won't stop crying, and I don't know what to do. But the worst thing, Lord, is that I am not happy being a mother. I feel so awful about this because I really do love this little guy. Please help me be a better mom. Please help me to handle all these motherhood duties with some joy. And please, please help him to stop crying. Amen.

Something prompted my sister-in-law and my mother-in-law to come by that evening. There was no way to hide my swollen eyes and my frazzled state. I tearfully confessed my shortcomings as a mother and admitted my lack of appreciation for my new life as a parent. I felt especially bad about confessing this to my sister-in-law since she was pregnant with her first child. But they both listened and responded with the most comforting words. They told me this was normal and that these days would soon pass. Kolby was just in a "fussy" spell and would soon return to his normal contented self. Thankfully, they were right.

The fussy afternoons slowly subsided, and Kolby continued to grow into a little person. His twinkly eyes and captivating smiles melted my heart daily. After a few months, his head was covered with curls and his almond-shaped eyes sparkled with mischief. As he neared the age of one, a walking, almost talking little person, I could truly say that I loved being a mother.

He has so much personality already. What is Your plan for him, God?

As Kolby entered the terrible twos, his mischievous side took the lead and challenged our untrained parenting skills to their limits. He was not the slightest bit shy or afraid of anything. He loved to run off, without a care as to where he was going, despite Kim and me urgently calling him to come back and stay close to us. His independent and outgoing personality would turn out to be a huge strength later on in his life, but it took a few years before we could appreciate these traits.

YOUR STORY:

Parenthood

THINKING BACK

- Did you plan or hope to be a parent before it happened in your life? Did you feel ready?
- Were there any preparations or discussions that helped or hindered your readiness for this new phase of life?

THINKING INWARD

- What feelings or emotions did you experience prior to parenthood?
- What were the greatest joys and the greatest challenges you faced as you adjusted to the new life of parenthood?

THINKING OUTWARD

- How did you choose your child's name? Did family members influence the choice?
- How soon did you notice unique personality traits in your child? Did you recognize traits that were similar to other family members?

THINKING FORWARD

- How has parenthood moulded the person you are today?
- What is your greatest hope for your parenthood role of the future?

Write a Prayer: What do you need help with, in your role as a parent? Bring every detail, question, and concern to God today.

Dear Heavenly Father,

Your word says that "Children are a heritage from the LORD, offspring a reward from him" (Psalm 127:3). I pray Your continued blessing, dear Lord, on every reader who has experienced this gift from You. I pray that You would guide them in their parenting role and in their relationships with their children. If anyone is experiencing postpartum depression, or other parenthood challenges, I pray that they would find help and that You would bring them relief. I also lift up to You, Lord, those who have not received the gift of children or have lost the gift by miscarriage or other events. Bring Your comfort and peace to them, I pray, as only You can.

In Your name, amen.

"My frame was not hidden from you
when I was made in the secret place,
when I was woven together in the depths of the earth.
Your eyes saw my unformed body;
all the days ordained for me were written in your book
before one of them came to be."

PSALM 139:15–16

CHAPTER 7
Optimistic

The timing could not have been worse. I was in Quebec on a summer course when I discovered I was pregnant again. It wasn't an accident—we had planned this. Kolby was two years old, and it seemed like the right time to add another little one to our family. But the timing of this pregnancy was not lining up with other circumstances in our lives.

Before I even had a chance to phone Kim and tell him about the positive pregnancy test, he called me with his exciting news. A ball team from Auckland, New Zealand, contacted him, inviting him to come and play there for the winter.

This was something we dreamed about and had talked about doing for quite a while. Kim had a ball player friend who had done this, so we were trying to find other contacts in New Zealand who might also be interested in hosting a Canadian fastball pitcher. He had not found a team that was interested in hosting us until now. A team from the large city of Auckland in the North Island called Kim, offering to host us. They would provide jobs, a place to live, and a car. This was a dream come true, exactly what we had been hoping for.

How can this be happening now? Why didn't this call come sooner?

After Kim shared all the exciting details, he noticed that I was not expressing any excitement. I hesitated. This did not feel like the right time to share the news about the pregnancy, but I couldn't keep it to myself. I blurted out the news. Kim was genuinely happy about the pregnancy too, so we just continued the phone conversation about my news, putting his news aside for the moment.

We had been trying to conceive our second child, but I had no idea when I left for Quebec that we were expecting. Both Kim's news and my news were the desires of our hearts, but the timing of the two events could not have been worse. We had a lot to talk about when I got home, and a lot of praying to do.

As soon as I hung up the phone, I shared my confused excitement with God.

Dear Lord, You have been so good to us. I can't thank You enough for all of Your great blessings to our little family. You have been with us through everything in our lives so far. You have blessed all aspects of our union and given us the gift of our precious son, Kolby. I am so grateful that You have chosen to bless us with another child. But the timing doesn't make sense, Lord. We have been hoping for this opportunity to go to New Zealand, and now it has finally come. Should we go, Lord, or are You showing us by this pregnancy that we shouldn't go? I know that Your perfect plan for us continues, and so I pray for Your guidance, Lord. Please help us make the right decision about this opportunity. Thank You, Lord. Amen.

We didn't sense God saying "yes," but we didn't feel He was saying "no" either. We decided the pregnancy didn't need to prevent us from fulfilling our desire to experience New Zealand and live there for the winter. They had a good quality health care system. As long as I could find a doctor, all would be well.

Why can't I have a healthy pregnancy there just as I would in Canada?

We decided the timing might work for me to have the baby there, and we could travel back home with a newborn "kiwi." So, with huge naivety and optimism, we booked our flights and made our plans to leave our life on the farm in rural Saskatchewan for seven months.

We had no idea what life would be like in the massive city of Auckland, NZ, but the lure of the adventure was stronger than our anxious thoughts. We could not help but wonder, however, if this adventure would work with a challenging two-year-old, a pregnancy, and many unknowns about the ball team people, the city, and the country. I continued to pray for direction.

The day of departure arrived, and we boarded the first plane, holding tight to Kolby. He was clinging to the new toy that his auntie had given him before we left. It was a "pull the string and listen to the farm animal sounds" toy. I'm sure the entire airplane wanted to chuck that toy out the window as we endured those farm sounds most of the long flight to New Zealand.

The host of the NZ ball team appeared apprehensive as she met us at the airport in Auckland. She was expecting the third member of our family, our busy little toddler, but she was not expecting the fourth member already showing on my growing midsection. Since they had not yet found a place for us to stay as promised, our little family with growing needs posed some problems.

She took us home to her house, and we settled there temporarily. My allergy to her cats, however, caused some issues, and my health deteriorated. I was having difficulty breathing due to sinus congestion from the allergies. I had no appetite but forced myself to stuff down a bit of yogurt each meal. After two weeks, the team still hadn't found a place for us to live, so she moved us to her mother's house. Despite the kindness of the elderly lady, it was obvious that she was not thrilled about hosting a family with a busy toddler in her home.

If only the team would come through with their promise to get us our own place. We need some space and different food. I am never eating yogurt again.

Six weeks after arriving in Auckland, we found our own flat to rent, and with donated second-hand furniture from the ball team, we finally had a place of our own that we could call home. Kim found an old Toyota that was affordable, so we now had some independence with our NZ life. I was hired to teach at a private school, and Kim was provided with work at a pharmaceutical warehouse.

Despite the pregnancy, I lost over ten pounds that month due to stress and allergies, but with our lifestyle more settled, I started to feel better. For the first time since we arrived, I made it through a whole day without tears.

We are going to be okay now. This adventure is going to turn out fine.

I remember telling Kim that everything was going to get better now that we had our NZ life details all in place. We were going to enjoy this new life experience with no more stress.

My fresh new optimism only lasted one day.

YOUR STORY:

New Opportunities

THINKING BACK

- Have you experienced the opportunity for travel or a new adventure? How did this opportunity come to you?
- What other factors in your life had to be considered before you moved forward with your adventure plans?

THINKING INWARD

- What internal guiding factors led you to your final decision about the new opportunity?
- What were the emotional highs or lows of your experience?

THINKING OUTWARD

- Did family members or friends influence your ideas about the opportunity?
- Were there any unexpected experiences or challenges from the people you met during your venture?

THINKING FORWARD

- How have your past experiences shaped your plans and desires for the future? If you could do it over again in the future, would you?
- Do you have travel plans or desires for adventure in the future?

Write a Prayer: Commit all your questions, concerns, and desires for travel or adventure to God today.

Dear Heavenly Father,

It is hard to understand why doors open or close when they do. It is also unexplainable where our internal desires come from and how they lead us to the decisions we make. I pray, dear Lord, that You would help us to see how You are at the helm of opening or closing doors. I lift up readers to You, Lord, who are reflecting on past ventures and wondering about the role they played in their lives. If any are contemplating a new adventure today, Lord, guide them with Your divine clarity.

In Your name, amen.

"The LORD makes firm the steps of the one who delights in him; though he may stumble, he will not fall, for the LORD upholds him with his hand."

PSALM 37:23–24

CHAPTER 8

Encouraged

No more tears. I am not going to waste one more minute crying over our decision to come here.

For the first time since we arrived in Auckland, NZ, I finally felt a bit of peace. It had taken almost two months, but we had our own place, jobs, and a bit of a routine. I could now choose and cook familiar food and regain my state of health. We could create more of a home environment for Kolby, and his behaviour would improve. We were going to be fine. That settled feeling lasted a mere 24 hours.

The very next day I was running after Kolby as he was chasing a ball on our friend's driveway. I tripped and fell hard against the side of a parked car. Piercing pains jolted through my left arm and I knew that something was terribly wrong. Our friend called Kim, and he rushed me to the hospital.

After many painful examinations and awkward X-rays, they realized my arm was broken in five places. I also had extensive nerve and ligament damage. This was not good news for anyone, but especially bad news for a pregnant woman with a toddler. The doctor was distraught but sympathetic as he explained that he was not sure what to do about my injury. They did not want to put a cast on the arm since this would require more X-rays, and X-rays were to be avoided as much as possible due to the pregnancy.

I was in extreme pain and could hardly pray, but I whispered desperate prayers that fateful day, asking God to give the doctor wisdom to make the right decision about my arm.

Dear Lord, why did this happen? I am in so much pain. My doctor doesn't even know what to do with me. Please guide him, Lord. Help him to figure out what to do with my arm. And please protect the little one in my womb. Amen.

A few hours later, the doctor returned. He had decided it would be better to put a steel plate in my arm to hold it together while it healed. With sincere regret, the sophisticated Auckland doctor warned me that due to the scars, I would probably not be able to wear strapless gowns in the future. I appreciated the irony of this comment later, thinking about the lack of strapless gowns in my closet on our farm in rural Saskatchewan. This was the least of my worries as I was admitted to the hospital in preparation for the surgery.

With my arm all bandaged up and in traction, the decision to give up my teaching position in Auckland was an obvious one. The teaching job had been a stressful and challenging position from day one. Dropping Kolby off at a daycare that he didn't like added more misery to each day. It was a relief to give up the teaching job and the spot at the daycare. Both Kolby and I were happy to close those doors.

Unfortunately, when I got home from the hospital, the days in the flat were long and difficult. Keeping Kolby entertained was challenging. He was frustrated, lonely, and bored and did not understand that Mommy couldn't do much with her growing tummy and painful arm. Not understanding my predicament, he would often hit and tug at my painful arm. Sending him to his room for a "time out" frustrated him even more. He pulled every page out of every book in his room and scribbled on the walls.

In desperation, I tried the reverse, locking myself in my bedroom, telling Kolby I wasn't coming out till he calmed down and quit hurting Mommy's arm. This actually worked for a few days. Kolby begged me to come out, promising to be good.

Life in Auckland felt like an ongoing bad dream that was just getting worse every day. My prayers were very short and to the point on those days.

Lord, please help me get through this day.

We had attended a church up the hill from our flat one Sunday just before my arm accident happened. We met a few people after the church service, but conversations had been short. One woman, with a son similar to Kolby's age, offered her help. She handed us a paper with her phone number. While I was in the hospital, Kim was in desperate need of help with Kolby. He remembered the kind offer from the woman at that church and decided to contact her. The woman consented to babysit Kolby in the afternoons for a few days.

The kind mom shared the story of my badly broken arm and our busy toddler with other church ladies. Much to our incredible surprise, the church ladies brought us dinners when I came home from the hospital. For ten days in a row, someone from that Presbyterian church up the hill, which we attended only one time, showed up at our door with a lovely home-cooked dinner for the three of us. It was an unimaginable bright spot in each day and an unbelievable blessing during a dark and difficult time.

During one of the dinner deliveries, the woman who brought the food noticed that I was completely overwhelmed trying to look after my difficult toddler while still in quite a bit of pain with my arm in traction. She had connections with Social Services of Auckland and thought that we might qualify for some paid childcare. Within a few days, a friendly female student had been hired for us. She showed up after school to take Kolby to the park. It was a gift straight from heaven for Kolby to have someone come to play with him every day for the next few weeks. For me, it was desperately needed relief to have a few hours of peace, quiet, and rest.

I hadn't even thought to pray for help like this. I was too over-whelmed and exhausted to pray effectively over our pathetic situation. But family back in Canada had heard about our difficult time on the other side of the world. My mom was praying along with many other relatives and church friends. God knew exactly what was going on in our lives in New Zealand, and He sent the help we needed to survive our days there.

It soon became obvious that having the baby in New Zealand was going to pose even more challenges. My arm was still in traction, and I really needed the support and help of family back home. Kim's mom and dad had already planned to come and visit us and tour around NZ for a few weeks, so we decided that Kolby and I would travel back home with them. Kim would stay two more months and complete his contract with the ball team. He could still get home in time for the birth of the baby if all went well. The trip home went smoothly thanks to the help of Mom and Dad Barnstable.

I'll never forget the morning our plane arrived in Calgary. It was the end of February and the sun was shining, yet it was lightly snowing. I had not yet seen snow that winter, and as I peered out the window of our plane that had just landed, I saw the wispy, white flakes with new eyes. Every snowflake danced and sparkled in the sunlight. The winter scene was magical. I had a whole new appreciation for Canada and realized more than ever what a beautiful and blessed place it was to live.

Thank You, God, from the bottom of my heart for our wonderful country of Canada.

Arriving back at our ranch-style home in the country was just as magical. It was so peaceful, quiet, and safe. I felt like a queen in a castle as I looked around our spacious home with quality furniture and appliances. Oh, how I had missed my La-Z-Boy recliner during the painful nights in Auckland! And then there was the bliss of our king-size waterbed. I would finally be able to get a good night's sleep. Our garage sale furniture in the Auckland flat had not provided any of the comforts I so badly needed with my wrecked arm and my uncomfortable pregnant body.

How can I sufficiently thank You, God, for my luxurious comfortable home in Canada?

Kolby was just as excited as I was to return home. His face lit up as he rediscovered every toy he had forgotten. He played contentedly for hours with his farm set, driving his little tractors with cultivators over the couch cushions as if every cushion was a field that urgently needed cultivating. Kim's dad brought the mail and checked on us every day. His mom called every evening to make sure we were okay.

The pregnancy continued to the final due date and beyond. I had been several weeks overdue with Kolby and it was happening again. This baby was in no hurry to arrive, but I was not impatient this time. I was more than grateful to have Kim arrive home with time to settle into life with us again before the baby was born. We had a few weeks of "normal" before our family would grow and our next stage of family life would begin.

Your timing is perfect, Lord. Thank You for holding on to this baby.

YOUR STORY:

Prayer Needed

THINKING BACK

- Can you recall a time in your life when you were facing a trauma and needed support?
- How long did it take before you received support and had relief? What made the difference?

THINKING INWARD

- How did the trauma affect your mental state? How did you cope with the trauma?
- Was anyone praying for you? If so, did you have a sense they were praying for you?

THINKING OUTWARD

- What role did the doctors and health care specialists play in your diagnosis and/or your treatment?
- Did any other people bring comforts or periods of relief during this difficult season in your life?

THINKING FORWARD

- Can you recall a prayer prayed over you in the past that has affected your future?
- If you had a personal prayer warrior praying for your future, what would be the focus of their prayers for you?

Write a Prayer: Can you think of someone today who is in desperate need of your prayers? Write a prayer for them.

Dear Heavenly Father,

I lift up readers who are experiencing trauma or pain today. I ask, dear Lord, that You bring healing and relief. Be very near to them, Lord, and help them to know that You have not forsaken them. If there are medical professionals involved, I ask that You give them Your wisdom to know the best treatment possible. May they make decisions that are guided by You to bring healing to the minds and the bodies of readers, I pray.

In Your name, Jesus, amen.

"This is what the LORD, the God of your father David, says: I have heard your prayer and seen your tears; I will heal you."

2 KINGS 20:5

CHAPTER 9

Conflicted

Apart from the trauma of my broken arm and the temporary weight loss, my second pregnancy didn't feel any different than my first one. Neither my health nor the position of the baby gave me any physical clues about whether the baby in my womb was a boy or a girl. No baby names were selected—until the dream.

While we were still living in New Zealand, I had a vivid dream about the birth of the baby. The baby in the dream was a girl, and we named her Key-aura. The word "kia ora" was a greeting word that meant "hello" or "welcome" in Maori, the native language of New Zealand. I hadn't thought about this word as a name before. I was thrilled about the idea when I woke up. I was now convinced that our unborn child was a girl. Not only was her first name decided, her middle name was going to be Marene, a combination of the names Mary, my mom, and Helene, Kim's mom.

Kiora Marene Barnstable … how lovely.

Much to my surprise, when the baby arrived on April 6, he was a boy! Even Kolby was not sure about this and asked, "Is my brother a boy or a girl?"

Another surprise for me was how I felt about this. I had the same euphoria about this little boy I had experienced at the birth of Kolby. I sensed God telling me that two boys in our family was just right and that a brother for Kolby was all a part of His perfect plan. The hard part now was coming up with a good name. We started praying for an original name that might have as much character as the girl's name we loved.

We finally settled on a unique name that Kim spotted in a sports article about a football player's son. The name was Kraymer. We then chose the name Jefferson for our second son's middle name. This unique name came from our boys' great-grandpa Barnstable, a gentle natured man with a fun-loving spirit.

Kraymer Jefferson Barnstable … a mouthful, but it does have character.

Little did we know that the name Kraymer would become very well-known through a popular half-hour comedy show not yet on TV named *Seinfeld*. Cosmo Kramer was a bizarre character known for his eccentric ideas and flamboyant actions. Fortunately, our Kraymer has always loved this show and has embraced the uniqueness of both of his given names.

Much like the character named Cosmo Kraymer on *Seinfeld*, our second son loved to make us laugh. He was a gentle, easygoing, fun-loving child right from the start. As we recall his childhood, we have fewer stories to tell, since his behaviour didn't push our parenting skills like our first son's. When he was asked to stop doing something, he would not challenge us with "why," "why," "why" questions like his brother did but would usually reply, "Okay, Mommy." Raising him seemed effortless most days. Many of our pictures show him baring a silly grin or in the middle of some crazy antics for the sake of a little humour.

When Kraymer was preschool age, Kim was playing a competitive level of fastball in Regina, so we often travelled on weekends for his tournaments. Kolby had almost grown up at the ballpark, and so it was a familiar place for him with lots to do. In Regina, he could chase after foul balls and earn a quarter for returning them to the sound box. Kraymer usually just settled in the stands beside me and was content to watch the game and nibble on sunflower seeds. One afternoon, another ball wife asked him if he wouldn't like to chase after foul balls along with the other boys.

"No thanks," Kraymer replied, "I'm not a running around kind of kid; I'm just a relaxed kind of kid."

While still at a young age, Kraymer had an intuitive ability to understand himself, as well as the people around him. When I was upset or troubled but not saying anything about it, Kraymer was the first to notice. He would ask me out of the blue what was wrong. In his later years, he casually made statements about people that perfectly summed up who they were or what they were dealing with.

What is Your plan for this boy, God? He is so uniquely gifted.

Both of our boys inherited their father's love for sports, and hockey became their full focus in the winter months. Kim created a small hockey arena in the basement of our home so the boys could play to their hearts' content. Kolby loved to shoot on the net, so Kraymer was instructed by big brother to stand there and try to block the shots. He was content to do this and became the goalie of choice for his brother and his cousins as they played mini hockey games for hours in the basements of our homes.

As the boys found their place on minor hockey teams, Kraymer continued to practice goaltending. His uncle coached him for novice hockey and usually allowed Kraymer to be the goalie since he wasn't a very strong skater. Unlike most players, Kraymer wanted to be in the net, so that became his most common position.

As Kraymer spent many hours in the net, his skill and technique continued to improve. Even before he reached bantam level, he was playing for the best team in the province. He was drafted to the WHL at the tender age of 15. His unique name, Kraymer Jefferson Barnstable, made the top 10 list of the most original names of players in the WHL and was listed as a top name in the Canadian university league, a point of great pride for our son.

Being a goalie, however, brought many trials. When your team wins, you are the hero, but when the team loses, you are the "goat," often taking full blame for the loss. Goalies were traded by teams and shifted around like worthless objects. Kraymer became a "human suitcase," playing for more teams and leagues than most aspiring hockey players.

He had to live wherever the team assigned him to live, which meant he was billeted in all kinds of homes. Many of these billet homes were not well screened and did not provide a good environment for a young man who needed life guidance to help him deal with the pressures of the hockey world.

Every time Kraymer was traded, my heart knotted up with worry and concern. *Where will he have to go? What kind of team and living situation will he have to adjust to this time? Should we put a stop to this, God, and save our son from this difficult life?*

We agonized over this decision, wondering if we had made a terrible mistake allowing Kraymer to continue playing this position or even to continue pursuing his seemingly unreachable hockey dream. Each time the agony of goalie parenting resurged, I tried to commit the anguish to God in prayer.

Dear Lord, how can I sufficiently thank You for my youngest son? You created him so unique and special. His personality is so relaxed and easy, his sensitivity to others and their feelings so caring and genuine. Sometimes, the world of hockey is just the opposite, so ruthless and mean. It seems like the wrong place for our son. Please guide us in our parenting, Lord. Please direct our decisions about whether or not to encourage our son to continue pursuing his hockey dreams. Thank You, Lord, that You have a perfect plan for his life and that You will never leave him or forsake him no matter where he is or what he is doing. I'm so grateful, Lord, that You are the engineer of his life. Amen.

It didn't make any sense at the time, but I felt that God was telling me something when I prayed. It seemed God was saying we should pay even more attention to Kraymer's hockey success. At the time, we were more focused on Kolby's hockey potential since he had more skill and even more passion for the sport. Putting more attention, time, and focus on Kraymer's hockey seemed like an odd choice.

We had no idea at the time that our youngest son's hockey experiences would lead him to a unique business and a career in the world of hockey.

YOUR STORY:

Difficult Decisions

THINKING BACK
- Have you faced difficult decisions for family members that had the potential to affect their future?
- What were the choices you had to make? What made the decisions challenging for you?

THINKING INWARD
- Have you experienced conflicting emotions about a family member's natural tendencies or abilities versus your preferred choices for them?
- What fears did you have about the choices you had to make or the choices they were making?

THINKING OUTWARD
- Did anyone in your family member's sphere of influence (i.e., friends, teachers, or coaches) play a role in identifying or developing their interests?
- Did you notice any God-given signs that seemed to point their lives in a certain direction?

THINKING FORWARD
- Are you facing a decision or dilemma that may impact a family member's future today?
- What is your greatest hope, desire, and prayer for your family today?

Write a Prayer: Ask God to give you a glimpse of His plan for your family member. Turn your trust over to Him and His perfect plan for their life.

Dear Heavenly Father,

You truly understand the love and concern that a parent has for their family. You placed that in us. You are well aware of the heavy responsibilities we face daily as we care for and make decisions for family members. As parents, Lord, we are in desperate need of Your wisdom to guide and direct us. I lift up to You now, dear Lord, all difficult choices and decisions regarding our family that we agonize over today. Give us divine guidance, I pray, and help us to leave our loved one's future in Your capable hands.

In Your name, amen.

"If any of you lacks wisdom, you should ask God,
who gives generously to all without finding fault,
and it will be given to you."

JAMES 1:5

CHAPTER 10
Pleading

The small crowd of fans cheered with over-the-top enthusiasm. You would have thought it was an Olympic game between Canada and the US with the gold medal at stake. Not quite. The opposing teams came from Canada and the US, but it was just a tournament of eight- and nine-year-old boys cheered on by their overly exuberant families.

Kolby was one of our star players. He played offence and moved around the ice like a future NHL star. He had all the drive and ambition of a future Gretzky. He was gifted with natural leadership skills and rallied the team, time after time, with his "give it all you got" attitude. He was passionate about the game, and it seemed he had the skill and the personality to go all the way. But the tournament in the US became a fateful weekend that cast a dark shadow on our firstborn son's hopes and dreams.

The weekend tournament started with Kolby enjoying his usual success on the ice, scoring many goals and leading our team to a possible championship. But discomfort in his hip was slowing him down, and his shifts on the ice became shorter and shorter. Finally, Coach Dad had to stop him from playing altogether. Kolby was just in too much pain.

What is going on with our son? This pain must be serious. Nothing has ever stopped him from playing hockey before.

We took our young athlete to the doctor as soon as possible and then to several specialists, but the medical system left us frustrated and disappointed. The doctors were baffled. There did not seem to be any obvious cause for the pain that Kolby was experiencing. X-rays did not reveal the issue. They put Kolby on the wait list for an MRI, but it was going to take at least seven long months. In total frustration, we looked at other options. Kim discovered we could get an MRI almost immediately in the US if we were willing to pay for it. We didn't have to think twice. As soon as we could, we headed to Minot, North Dakota, in hopes of finding out what was causing our son's pain.

Not only did we get an MRI right away in Minot, we finally got a diagnosis for Kolby's condition. We were told that he had Perthes Disease, a rare genetic hip disorder that caused his one hip joint to not function as it should. Instead of working like a ball in a socket, Kolby's hip bone had flattened right out and was grinding against the other bones in the socket. No wonder our boy was in pain.

The treatments offered for Perthes Disease were devastating. Most doctors recommended a leg brace that would prevent the hip from having any weight on it. This brace limited normal leg movement, and ramps would be needed in place of stairs. Just ordinary walking would be a challenge, let alone any sport activities or skating.

We could not even imagine Kolby in this brace. His passion in life was sports, and this brace would rob him of all that he loved for several years. It seemed too much for our boy to bear. I prayed earnestly for God to stop this from happening to our eldest son. In desperation, we took Kolby to a special service in Regina where a "faith healer" laid hands on our son and prayed for his healing. It seemed that nothing happened, but I continued to pray and plead for healing.

Dear Lord, You are the great healer. Your word states You are able to heal every disease and sickness. Father, it is so hard to understand why our firstborn son, with so much athletic ability, would be struck with this rare disease in his hip. You know him well, Lord, and You know his every hope and dream. You know all about his passion for sports, especially hockey. We pray for his healing, in Your name, Lord, and ask that You would restore the use of his hips and his legs so that he would be able to do what he loves. In Your powerful name we ask this, Lord. Amen.

Every time I prayed for Kolby's healing, the same verse kept coming to mind: "Now to him who is able to do immeasurably more than we ask or imagine, according his power that is at work within us" (Ephesians 3:20).

Before we could even settle into despair about the leg brace possibility, Kim heard about a doctor who had discovered another option for treating Perthes Disease. This orthopedic specialist, based in Saskatoon, had discovered that keeping the muscles around the hip joint strong was sometimes better than taking all the pressure off of the hip joint with the leg brace. This doctor was curious about Kolby's situation and agreed to see him right away. She believed that if Kolby faithfully completed the recommended physical therapy, he would be able to keep the hip strong enough to avoid the brace. This was definitely worth a try.

After more X-rays and careful examinations at her Saskatoon clinic, the doctor sent Kolby home with papers of pictures explaining and demonstrating how to do the physiotherapy on his own. But before she let him go, she asked him a crucial question.

"How are you doing in school?" she inquired. "What kind of grades do you get?"

"Not bad," Kolby replied, "I get mostly As." This was the truth. Kolby did extremely well in school. He was meticulous and detailed with schoolwork and always did his best.

"That's good to hear," the doctor responded. "Because you will need to choose a career that uses your mind instead of your body."

This turned out to be very valuable advice for our firstborn son.

Kolby managed to avoid that horrid brace by faithfully completing the exercises. He embraced the daily routine with his usual enthusiasm and optimistic attitude. He rarely complained about the pain and was able to keep up with his normal, active lifestyle.

When we prayed for Kolby, we envisioned a full healing of that hip. We wanted our son to have perfect body parts that would not hold him back in any physical pursuits. It seemed some days that our son limped a bit more than usual and our prayers had not been answered. But God did more than we realized. Our eldest son continued to enjoy playing ball, golf, and high levels of hockey.

Kolby went on to play midget AAA and played for several teams in junior A as well as for two college hockey teams. He continued to develop his mind in school and in college, graduating with a business degree. He has been using his entrepreneurial mind for sales, marketing, and leadership roles in his career.

YOUR STORY:

Healing Needed

THINKING BACK
- Have you ever had to face a health crisis in the life of a loved one?
- How did their trauma affect your life?

THINKING INWARD
- What were your beliefs around the causes or possible cures of the health challenge?
- What were your worries or fears around the long-term or residual effects of this health crisis?

THINKING OUTWARD
- What was your experience with medical professionals who were involved?
- Did the beliefs of family members or friends play a role in treatment options?

THINKING FORWARD
- What is your greatest concern about the future health of your loved ones?
- Do you fear that their lack of health will cause more hardship in the future?

Write a Prayer: Tell God your detailed concerns about the health of your loved ones. Ask Him to intervene in any health crisis they face.

Dear Heavenly Father,

Your word says "I am the LORD, who heals you" in Exodus 15:26 and "I will restore you to health and heal your wounds" in Jeremiah 30:17. There is no doubt that You have the power to heal and restore, yet this healing does not always come when or how we desire it. Help us, dear Lord, to understand Your ways and to trust that You are in control despite troubling circumstances. I pray for any reader today who is seeking healing for a loved one, and I ask, dear Lord, that You would answer their prayer and restore their loved ones to health. If You have a different plan, Lord, help the reader to know You have heard their prayers and You have not forsaken them.

In Your name, amen.

"He will call on me, and I will answer him;
I will be with him in trouble,
I will deliver him and honor him."

PSALM 91:15

CHAPTER 11

Suffering Loss

Halloween was usually a day I anticipated with a spirit of fun and frivolity. I could put together a silly costume and turn myself into a cartoon character or a bizarre creature for one whole day. It was the day when diet caution was thrown to the wind and mini chocolate bars and sugary treats could be indulged in to my heart's content.

But this Halloween was different. The entire atmosphere was eerie and depressing, and even though the air was still, it was hard to breathe. Unfortunately, the foreboding gloom of the day had nothing to do with the imaginary antics of October 31. The impending doom was a reality in my life that came from an unexpected and devastating phone call.

My dad was dying. They didn't know if he would survive one more day.

It was four short months before when Dad experienced the first signs of a health problem. My mom and dad were returning from a trip to BC for a June wedding when Dad became very ill. By August, his doctor decided that surgery was needed to see what was happening inside his body. But the surgery accomplished nothing other than revealing some extremely tragic news. My dad had a fast-growing cancer that had already spread throughout his abdominal cavity. It was considered stage four. There was nothing they could do.

In desperation, Mom and Dad travelled to Mexico, hoping that alternative therapies might make a difference in Dad's diagnosis. They put Dad on a special diet and began to pump vitamins and minerals into him, but even the Mexican doctors admitted that it was too late for their therapies to be effective. After a few weeks, Mom and Dad returned home, realizing that Dad needed to be back in a comfortable Canadian environment before he became too sick to travel.

My three sisters and I received a phone call the evening of October 31 telling us to come home as soon as possible. I was hoping there was still a chance that I could see and talk to my dad one last time. I quickly threw some clothes in a suitcase, and Kim, Kolby, and I headed out on the longest and most disheartening four-hour drive home that we had ever experienced. Kolby slept peacefully in the back seat, unaware of the gloom in our quiet car. Conversation between Kim and I was sparse as we choked back tears. There were no words that could relieve the deep sadness of that Halloween night.

Life without Dad will never be the same.

My dad was a charismatic man, strong in personality and in stature. He was only five feet, ten inches tall, but he had an athletic, broad shouldered, and stocky build. He was a hardworking farmer most of his life. He also became a successful realtor in his later years, using his high-spirited nature to win over his clients. He longed for a son to help him with work on the farm and to share his love of hockey and sport vehicles, but the blessing of a son was not a part of God's plan. Our dad was disappointed at the births of his four children as each one turned out to be a girl. But over the years, he showed more and more appreciation and great pride in the four daughters that God had chosen to give him.

It was past midnight by the time three of Farmer Brown's daughters arrived home and gathered around his bed. His breathing was laboured, and it was hard for him to talk, but he was able to see us and tell us how much he loved us. And then he admitted something that we didn't expect. Our strong and tough-minded dad told us that he knew he was dying but he was scared about how it would happen and how he would get to the other side. He asked us girls to pray for him.

We did our best to bring our dad's fears to God in prayer. The words didn't seem sufficient, but God knew our hearts, and, more importantly, He knew the state of Dad's heart. Before the morning light of November 1 arrived, our dad, Cornelius David Brown, went to be with his Lord and Saviour in heaven. He was only 59 years old.

Our mom was 55 years young when she became a widow. Despite her limited knowledge of finance details, Mom took over the financial decisions with wisdom beyond her experiences. She made wise investments and built a dream home that our family was able to enjoy whenever we came home. She entertained friends and relatives with grace and style, even though cooking was not her favourite thing to do. She was a beautiful woman, inside and out, with a caring, gentle nature that was loved and appreciated by all who had the chance to know her.

Less than ten years after our dad died, our precious mom was diagnosed with breast cancer. Losing our dad to cancer so young felt wrong and totally unjust. It seemed even more unthinkable now that Mom would have to battle cancer too.

Please don't take her too, God. We need our mom.

Mom had learned a tremendous amount of information about natural methods of fighting cancer during Dad's illness, so when chemotherapy didn't seem to be working, she decided to try an alternative route as well. Unfortunately, it seemed to prolong her battle. Her fight against breast cancer was long and painfully difficult. My three sisters and I tried to help Mom as best we could. For me, it required that four-hour drive on the weekends to be with her.

She was hospitalized the last few months of her life, and her pain was managed with high doses of morphine. On her good days, we tried to capture the essence of our mom's life by asking her key questions about life experiences she had never told us about. She loved the questions, but her foggy mind had trouble giving us clear answers.

If only we had started collecting her memories sooner.

Eventually her mind and her body no longer had good days. My sisters and I began to pray that her suffering would end and that she could just go to heaven. Our dear mother, Mary (Funk) Brown, finally gave up her battle with cancer in May 1998. By the time Mom left this earth, we were relieved that her painful days were over. She would receive a new and perfect body and be reunited with Dad in heaven.

Two of my sisters and I were married with families of our own at the time, but we all felt like orphans with no parents left on earth to guide us with our life decisions.

YOUR STORY:
Losing a Loved One

THINKING BACK

- Have you experienced the loss of one or both of your parents? Where were you and what was happening in your life when you received the devastating news?
- How was your life affected when you no longer had a parent to turn to?

THINKING INWARD

- Were you able to have last months, days, or moments with your dying parent? What emotions or feelings were expressed?
- If you could just call them and share your thoughts with them today, what would you say?

THINKING OUTWARD

- Have other members of your family been equally as impacted by the loss of your parent(s) as you?
- What is your most cherished memory of your parent(s)? How can you keep this memory alive in your family?

THINKING FORWARD

- What belief systems or legacy did your parent(s) leave for you?
- What is your greatest hope and prayer for your own legacy as you accept the responsibilities of your generation?

Write a Prayer: Tell God your every question about losses in your life that have affected you deeply. Ask Him to give you a glimpse of why this happened.

Dear Heavenly Father,

You know and understand the deep sorrow that comes from the loss of a father or a mother. It leaves us with a hole in our hearts that feels like it will never heal. It changes us. I pray for my readers today, Lord, who have experienced this life-impacting loss along with me, and I pray for every reader who is suffering the too-soon tragic loss of a parent. Comfort us, dear Lord, as only You can, and help us to lean on You as our loving Father. Help us to let go of anger or bitterness from this loss and be filled with love, patience, and understanding. May the best traits of our parents rise to the top in our lives so that we may pass on this heritage to our families.

In Your name, amen.

"If I go and prepare a place for you,
I will come back and take you to be with me
that you also may be where I am."

JOHN 14:3

CHAPTER 12

Seeking

My car chugged wearily up the hill toward the school where I was teaching. It was nearly out of gas, and so was I. I tried to recall the days when I loved teaching and felt passion towards my chosen career. It was a distant memory now, an irretrievable feeling. I wasn't sure how or why it happened, but my satisfaction with the profession of teaching had completely fizzled.

It was my twelfth year of teaching when I hit this wall of teacher burnout. I had just completed another contract with the Saskatchewan Ministry of Education, revising the French curriculum for grades 9 to 12 and training new teachers at this level. With this additional work on the side now complete, I returned to the basics of regular classroom teaching, but my motivation to teach had completely faded. Like a helium balloon that had lost its air, I felt flat and completely void of the energy needed to enter my classroom and face my students, day after day. I looked outside the window of my classroom with longing.

Will I ever get my love for teaching back? What kind of work could I do outside of a school?

I noticed that other teachers with a master's degree were learning new strategies and finding new opportunities. Maybe further studies could relight the spark of teaching for me. I looked into program options and made the decision to enrol in courses for a master's degree through distance learning at Athabasca University. But I didn't get far.

I had only completed two classes of my master's studies when our lives shifted. My mom had just been diagnosed with cancer, and the long journey of her battle was just beginning. I had to put my plans for a master's degree on the back burner, as my time and attention were needed elsewhere.

When Mom went to heaven, I took a year's leave of absence from teaching. I didn't fully realize it at the time, but I needed this year to recover from the trauma of Mom's suffering and the hardship of losing her. My mom had always been the person I could go to with my life questions and ponderings about spiritual confusion.

Since I now had more time each day, I began to seek God for hours every morning. I cried out to Him and expressed my feelings of being lost and alone without anyone to give me guidance. I asked God all of my "why" questions about our lives. I stayed in my prayer chair every morning until I received some type of "nugget" from God that would help me get through the day. I kept a prayer journal and recorded key points that I felt God was teaching me.

A few months after starting this prayer routine of seeking God earnestly every morning, I had the most unexpected experience. I was semi-awake in the middle of the night when I sensed that Jesus was present in our bedroom. It was around 4 a.m. He stood at the side of our bed, and an unexplainable calm filled the room as if this was an ordinary occurrence. I was filled with the presence of absolute peace and was not afraid or ashamed. It seemed like my typical prayer time, but with a clearer sense of who I was praying to.

The first thing Jesus said was that He had heard every one of the questions I had expressed in my prayers and that He had come to answer them. He encouraged me to simply ask Him again what I needed to know, and He would answer. Kim was fast asleep beside me, so I began to think of the deepest questions in my mind, and Jesus answered each one with clear and simple statements that needed no further explanation.

I asked dozens of "why" questions and "what will happen" questions about our lives and our families. Every answer seemed logical and brought peace and hope to my thoughts about our future.

Around 6 a.m., I needed to use the bathroom. I recall thinking that it would be just awful to interrupt this incredible conversation. Getting out of bed would probably end this amazing visit abruptly. But after a few minutes, the urgency of my situation could not be ignored, and I had to say, "Excuse me, Jesus, I need to use the bathroom," and I scurried out of bed as quickly as I could. Turning the light on in my ensuite bathroom, I knew I was fully awake. I realized how unbelievable and extraordinary this visit with Jesus was and kept hoping that my bathroom break had not caused it to end. I hurriedly jumped back into bed and snuggled under the covers once again.

The presence of Jesus returned instantly, and the conversation continued as if it had not been interrupted. About a half-hour later, I finally ran out of questions to ask. Jesus instructed me to rest now and to call upon Him and to seek Him directly for help with future life decisions. I drifted back into a peaceful sleep, with no full understanding yet that I had just experienced a most incredible visit with almighty God Himself in the flesh.

When I woke up to the alarm at 7:30, my first thought was that I had just dreamed the most wonderful dream. But as I recalled the details of the nighttime visit with Jesus, I remembered being fully awake when using the washroom at 6 a.m. yet continuing to talk with Jesus when I got back to bed. I was so thankful for the reality check of the bathroom break, since it was wide-awake evidence that Jesus had actually been in the room with me. It wasn't a dream.

I tried to tell Kim about the incredible vision, but it was almost too much for him to take in. I decided that I would write the facts of the vision down on paper while they were clear in my mind. I could return to the details later and see if what Jesus had told me still made sense.

One of the key messages that Jesus shared with me was that there would be a huge change coming in our lives. This change would be difficult for our two boys at first, but it was all a part of God's plan for their lives. We were not to worry about them; we should just keep moving forward according to doors that would open one at a time.

Even though it all seemed logical and clear during the vision, the answers that Jesus had shared with me brought many more questions later.

What kind of change will our family encounter?

Why do I feel so restless about teaching?

What will I do if I give up my teaching job?

Why should I pay attention to portfolios?

What will happen to Kolby's hip as he gets older?

Why is hockey more important for Kraymer's future?

Will farming continue to be the main focus of Kim's career? If not, what will be our main source of income?

I continued to ask God these questions in my future prayers, just as He had instructed me to do.

YOUR STORY:

A Spiritual Experience

THINKING BACK

- Have you ever had a spiritual encounter? Did it seem like a dream, a vision or an actual visit with a heavenly being?
- What was happening in your life before this encounter came about? Were you seeking God or guidance of some kind before it happened?

THINKING INWARD

- What emotions did you experience with this encounter? Did it bring fear and confusion or satisfaction and peace?
- Did you doubt the validity of your spiritual encounter? What led you to the conclusions you now have about this encounter?

THINKING OUTWARD

- Did you share this experience with anyone? If so, what was their reaction?
- Have you heard of or read about others who have had some type of divine visit? How did it impact their lives?

THINKING FORWARD

- What can we learn from characters in the Bible who have had visions or dreams? How did it affect their future?
- Have you ever asked God to reveal Himself to you through a vision or dream? Can you prepare for this?

Write a Prayer: If you were to have the privilege of a visit from God Himself in the near future, what would you say to Him? Write down all the questions that come to your mind.

Dear Heavenly Father,

Many characters in the Bible experienced dreams or visions that came from You. Daniel had dreams and visions that foretold the future (Daniel 7:1–3). Joseph, the father of Jesus, was instructed through the visit of an angel in a dream (Matthew 1:20). That is only two; there are other stories of how You have spoken to Your people in dreams and visions. I pray a blessing on every reader who has experienced this type of encounter and ask that You would remove all doubt about it and verify the reality of their divine encounter. I also pray, dear Lord, for every reader who craves to hear from You. Make Yourself known to us, I ask, and continue to answer our questions about life and Your divine plans for us.

In Your name, amen.

"For God does speak—now one way, now another—though no one perceives it. In a dream, in a vision of the night, when deep sleep falls on people as they slumber in their beds."

JOB 33:14–15

CHAPTER 13
Restless

My thoughts tossed and turned like a raft in the middle of an ocean storm. Several years had passed since my divine encounter. My nighttime visit with Jesus Himself that had answered all my questions about life and given me a sense of peace about my future at the time was now a foggy memory. I tried desperately to recall that state of peace and contentment, but it seemed so long ago. Life's routine had continued, and the ordinary days, months, and years of our lives in rural Saskatchewan had moved forward in a predictable pattern. I should have felt peace and contentment with all my blessings, but I didn't. I just felt restless.

Why am I so restless? What change do I desire? I can't even describe what I want.

After my leave of absence from teaching, I still had no desire to go back into the classroom. I started doing contract work in training and consulting for the regional college. I also accepted contract work with several other organizations, including the Post-Secondary Ministry of Education. I facilitated workshops on Prior Learning Assessment and Portfolio (PLAR) development for teachers and employment counsellors. These workshops took place all over the province and required continuous travel.

Travelling to the workshops was a huge novelty at first, but the travelling lifestyle did not work well with our family life. Kim and the boys longed for the good old days when Mom was a teacher and had a regular schedule that matched the boys' weekday lives. The irregularity of my work travel was wearing on me as well, and I began to crave a more predictable schedule.

Just as my PLAR contract was coming to a close, I heard they needed a French teacher once again at ECS, the high school where I had previously taught. The school district contacted me and offered me another teaching contract. It was somewhat of a relief to be back at my old school in the familiar place of teaching French, but it was also a bit disappointing. Every day brought feelings of "been here, done this," and that restless desire for a new and different challenge surged in me again. Kim was frustrated with me and my yearnings, and so I began to pray about my restless feelings. I prayed that I could just settle into the "bloom where you are planted" way of thinking.

Dear Lord, You are the almighty God, my creator, my saviour, and my friend. I am so grateful that You created me the way I am for a reason. You know me so well. You know the number of hairs on my head. You have a plan for me and the lives of my family that goes beyond our understanding. Lord, You know very well the state of my mind these days. I am so restless, and I don't know why. Kim is wishing I could be happy with where we are, doing what we do, but I can't seem to settle into this. Help me, dear Lord, to find contentment in my current situation and appreciate all that You have blessed us with in our lives here. Thank You, Lord. Amen.

My prayers were answered in a much different way than I expected.

Kim had been doing some sideline work as a scout for the Vancouver Giants hockey team at major hockey tournaments in Saskatchewan. Every fall, he travelled to Vancouver for the WHL team training camp. After his third year of taking part in this fall camp, he seemed different when he came home. Something had happened, but he wasn't ready to tell me.

After a few days of mulling it over, he finally admitted that the owners of the Giants team had told him something that really made him think. The staff of the team noticed that Kim had done a good job of scouting potential players for the team and recognized the value he brought to the organization. They mentioned that it would be great to involve him with other aspects of the team, but this would only be possible if Kim lived closer. A seed of yearning and restlessness was planted in Kim's mind that was impossible for him to ignore. It was that same seed of restlessness that had been growing in my mind for quite a while.

When Kim shared his feelings of restlessness and his desire to try a career in the world of hockey, I could hardly believe my ears. He had become just as restless as me, but at a much faster pace. Along with his restlessness, however, came a sense of despair and deep discontent. I could see the internal battle that was going on in his mind. This opportunity to have a career in hockey was exciting and luring, yet actually accepting the job was overwhelming and seemingly impossible.

The full view of Kim's internal conflict was not fully revealed to me, but I knew that he was in a state of serious inner turmoil over our future. As much as I didn't want to face it, I feared that there was even more to it than a career change. He was emotionally absent in our marriage, and his love for me seemed unexplainably blocked. Whenever worried thoughts for him and our marriage overcame my mind, I knelt down by his side of the bed and prayed for him and us.

Dear Lord, Your presence in our lives is undeniable. You have already led, guided, healed, and blessed us in so many ways. You know exactly what is going on in Kim's mind today. You know all about his restlessness and the desire that both of us have to try something new in our lives. You also know about the threat to our marriage that is making all of this even more complicated. Lord, I pray that You would protect us and help us move from this frustrating place of restlessness to the next place You have designed for us. I will try to leave all of these anxious thoughts with You now. In Your precious name I ask this. Amen.

Eventually, we faced the elephant in the room and started talking about the idea of moving our family to Vancouver. It seemed like a crazy and impossible mission to accomplish.

If our marriage is troubled now, will it survive this move? How in the world will Kim leave the family farm? How will the boys react to this huge change?

They were at the tender ages of 13 and 16, not exactly ideal times in their lives to remove them from everything comfortable and familiar.

Will Kim's family, so closely connected to our lives, be able to handle the idea of us moving two provinces away?

We decided to take the boys with us on a family holiday to BC during the Christmas holidays to explore this crazy idea.

Our family trip to BC didn't fully confirm that we should move to BC, but it did fuel the desire to move forward. Kim continued to talk with the staff of the Vancouver Giants and discuss employment options. I started investigating work opportunities that fit with my skills and experiences. We also looked at the housing market of Delta, school options for the boys, and, of course, hockey teams where they could play at their best level. The choices were endless and completely overwhelming.

At times all the decisions and work ahead of us seemed too overpowering. We often talked about just forgetting the whole idea. But something spurred us on to keep pursuing the move. The seed had been too firmly planted in both of our minds now, and we couldn't ignore it, despite our fears and the long list of hardships ahead of us.

YOUR STORY:

Lacking Peace

THINKING BACK

- Have you ever experienced long-term restless feelings but you didn't really know why? What were some possible causes?
- Did the restless state lead to a change in your life? How did the opportunity for change come about?

THINKING INWARD

- What emotions did you experience as you contemplated change? Did these feelings lead you forward or hold you back?
- How did you deal with your lack of peace as you were in the decision process? Did you share the feelings with anyone?

THINKING OUTWARD

- What other opinions or factors helped you to make the decision to move forward or to decide against the change?
- Did you receive any helpful advice or guidance from a family member or friend?

THINKING FORWARD

- If you faced a similar opportunity for change in the future, would you make the same decision?
- Are you expecting or hoping for major change opportunities in your life in the near future? What is your greatest desire regarding this change?

Write a Prayer: Tell God all about your restless feelings. Ask Him to either lead you forward or take the restlessness away according to His plan for your life.

Dear Heavenly Father,

It seems that You often lead us forward by allowing us to become restless with our current situation. Sometimes it leads to change, but sometimes it doesn't, Lord, so we ask for Your wisdom and guidance when we are dealing with these feelings. I pray for every reader who is feeling restless today or lacking peace in their present lives, dear Lord, and I ask that You would calm their restless angst or confirm that change is coming. For those who are hoping and looking for the next door to open, I pray that You would grant their desire, Lord, and lead them to the place You have planned for them to go.

In Your name, amen.

"The LORD himself goes before you and will be with you; he will never leave you nor forsake you. Do not be afraid; do not be discouraged."

DEUTERONOMY 31:8

CHAPTER 14
Guided

What kind of parents rip two teenage boys, at the sensitive ages of 13 and 16, from all that is comfortable and familiar and move them thousands of miles away to a new province, new city, new school, and completely new lifestyle? As we talked about all this with our boys, their reactions comforted us.

Kolby was fully on board with the plan. He saw the adventure in it and the chance to meet new people and make new friends. Imagine all of the "hot" girls in a large secondary school with over two thousand students, compared to his school in Estevan, Saskatchewan, with only a few hundred. Kraymer didn't really like change of any kind, so he was less enthused. He would be leaving his elementary school near our farm with fewer than 80 kids and starting grade eight in a strange and massive secondary school.

Both boys liked the idea of playing hockey at their best level without having to travel four to five hours, but they couldn't even imagine what this would be like. They naively co-operated with our plan, fully trusting their mom and dad to make the best decision for our family's future.

I prayed fervently for God to guide us to our next home and to the best location for the boys' lives.

Dear Father, You are the great "I Am," the almighty God who sees all and knows all. You are the master engineer of our lives, and Jeremiah

29:11 applies to our boys' lives too. You have plans to prosper their lives and not to harm them, plans to give them hope and a future. We are following what we think is Your plan for our whole family, Lord, moving to BC, but starting our lives over again in this new place is so overwhelming. Where should we look for a house, dear Lord? There are so many options. What secondary school in Delta is the best one for them? How will they find their hockey teams? Please guide us every step of the way, Lord. Please direct us to an area and a house that will be right for our boys. Thank you, Lord, that You hear and that You answer my prayers. I trust in You, Lord. Amen.

We had been looking at the homes for sale online all over Delta but we had no idea how to narrow down the choices. During our Christmas trip to Vancouver, through friends we came across some people who were thinking of selling their house in Ladner. Ladner seemed like a good fit for us, since it was a fishing and farming community with a small-town feel. We had a brief chance during our Christmas trip to walk through the house possibly coming up for sale. The owners had not fully decided what they were going to do.

Much to our surprise, the owners of the Ladner home contacted us in March and offered us the chance to purchase the home without the involvement of realtors if we agreed to their price. We didn't have time to travel to Vancouver for another look, but the house was much better quality than anything we had seen in that price range. After some urgent prayers and discussion of what we could remember about the home and the area, we committed to buying the house on Kensington Place over the phone. It felt a bit reckless and risky, but with an element of roll-the-dice excitement.

In April, I made the trip to Vancouver on my own for some interviews regarding job opportunities. I had the chance to look closely at this home we had purchased over the phone. This would be the house that would become our new home in three short months. The details of the house were not even clear in my mind from the first quick viewing, so I was nervous to see it again.

As I parked anxiously in front of the house, a flood of emotion washed over me. I loved it even more than the first time I saw it.

I can hardly believe this is going to be where we will live! This house has more curb appeal than I remember. How did I not notice the stunning front entry?

My first impression of the house had been favourable, but I had not allowed myself to look too closely since it wasn't even for sale at the time. This second look allowed me to fully take in every detail.

The first visual pleasure was the bright green grass and the flower gardens near the door with already blooming tulips, lilies, and pansies. It was pure delight for this girl from Saskatchewan, where grass and flowers were still buried under the last spring snowfall.

The black front door had elegant appeal with a stunning Japanese maple tree shading the entry and the front window. The front door opened to a grand foyer with a ceiling as high as the second floor. Right off the majestic foyer was a cozy living room with a gas fireplace on the back wall. The kitchen was fully open to a dining area and a small family room with another cozy fireplace. All the bedrooms were upstairs, including the master bedroom at end of the hall. It came equipped with a walk-in closet and an ensuite that beamed with rays of sun from the skylight overlooking the soaker tub.

It was a totally different type of house than our ranch-style home on the farm, but I could imagine our family living there. My heart skipped with extra beats of excitement and anticipation.

We searched through hundreds of homes looking for the best one for our family. This home found us, guided by You, God.

After the quick trip in April, I could hardly wait to move to Kensington Place in Ladner, BC. Thinking of our new home made the hard work of packing and emptying our house on the farm a little bit easier. I had several garage sales and did my best to de-clutter and purge our belongings that had been gathering there for 20 years.

Our marriage was still strained, but I pushed our issues to the back of my mind. There were moments, however, when the truth of what could happen to us could not be ignored. I privately faced the fear by asking myself if I would rather be divorced living in rural Saskatchewan or be a divorcee living in Greater Vancouver. The answer to that question propelled me to keep packing with even more fervour.

Selling our home on the acreage seemed too final, so despite the strain on our finances, we decided to rent it for a year. This would make our move to BC seem like a one-year trial and give us the option of coming back if we wanted to.

Now that we knew where we were going to live, we could move forward with registering the boys for school and investigating hockey teams for the fall. This unimaginable idea of starting our lives over in BC was actually falling into place.

YOUR STORY:

Taking a Risk

THINKING BACK

- Have you ever made a major decision where you had to rely on faith and make the choice without the full information? What initially led you to the final choice?
- What were the circumstances surrounding the decision? What were the potential advantages or disadvantages of the choices?

THINKING INWARD

- What emotions did you experience as you pushed yourself to rely on faith to make the decision?
- Did you use any internal strategies or ways of measuring gut feelings for making decisions like this?

THINKING OUTWARD

- Did family members or friends play a role in your decision?
- Did you have a chance to seek the advice of specialists in the field?

THINKING FORWARD

- Would you repeat this decision if a similar opportunity like this one arrived in your future?
- Will you be facing a difficult decision in your near future?

Write a Prayer: Tell God about past, present, or future decisions that are troubling your mind. Ask for His divine guidance and perspective.

Dear Heavenly Father,

Life comes with unavoidable decisions that we sometimes have to make without the luxury of time to investigate or contemplate the options. We need Your wisdom more than ever during those times, Lord, and so we ask for Your divine help and guidance. If any readers are in that precarious place today, Lord, I ask that You would help them to submit their worries to You and fully trust in You. Calm their fears, I pray, and point them in the direction of the best choice for them. Give them peace about the decision, Lord, with added assurance that You are directing their paths.

In Your name, amen.

"Trust in the LORD with all your heart
and lean not on your own understanding;
in all your ways submit to him,
and he will make your paths straight."

PROVERBS 3:5–6

CHAPTER 15

Surprised

He looked at me with big sad brown eyes as if he was reading my mind. I rubbed his furry head and scratched behind his ears just where he liked it. He lay contentedly at my feet and sighed a big heavy sigh. I exhaled a deep breath along with him, but my sigh ended with a gulp in my throat. My worries about what was going to happen to this huge and deeply loved furry member of our family dominated my thoughts. Daq, our Great Pyrenees dog, was one belonging that was impossible to pack or take with us to our new home in BC.

Daq had been a part of our family for four years. He accepted us and loved us from day one, quickly becoming a valuable member of our family. We adopted him from an elderly couple in a town nearby when he was several years old. His name meant "Norwegian warrior," and it suited him perfectly. He was a majestic and intimidating dog that fiercely protected our property from the first day he arrived. He patrolled the edges of our acreage and guarded us with instinctive loyalty.

As devastating as it was, we knew life in the city would not be a good choice for our massive pet. We had to find a new home and a new family for Daq. I asked around and called every neighbour who might be interested in owning this big, beautiful creature. No one was interested. Our family started to pray, asking God for His help with

Daq. This request was urgent because the time to leave Saskatchewan was getting close.

Dear Lord, I thank You that You care for every one of Your creations on earth. Your word says that not even a single sparrow can fall to the ground without You knowing about it (Matt. 10:29). So, I know, dear Lord, that You care about Daq and what happens to him. You created this majestic animal with strong protective instincts. Surely there is a place here in Saskatchewan where he will be appreciated and adored. Please direct us to find that new home for our precious Daq. Amen.

After many calls, I finally got a tip from a neighbour about a veterinarian who might consider taking Daq. He lived on an acreage about an hour and a half away from our farm. It took several tries to connect with the vet on the phone, but when I finally reached him, every try was worth it. The vet consented to taking our dog. He was a man of few words and didn't have time to give me much information. Minimal details were shared over the phone, other than scheduling the day and time for Daq's delivery.

The only other ride in a vehicle Daq had experienced was the day we picked him up four years before, so when Kim scooped him up and plopped him in the back of my SUV, his whole body shook. His big dark eyes were filled with fear as if he knew his life with us was over. Our faces were probably a dead giveaway, as all four of us were fighting back the tears unsuccessfully. We were an emotionally distraught group, each of us trying to mask our deep sorrow as Kim drove to the farm that would become Daq's new home.

As we pulled into the veterinarian's yard, we were greeted by the most unexpected surprise. Another beautiful Great Pyrenees dog, a female, ran out to the vehicle. As soon as we opened the back door, Daq jumped out of our SUV without hesitation. The two dogs circled and sniffed a gentle and accepting "hello." The veterinarian invited us to join him on his patio, which overlooked a vast and beautiful valley. As we sat on the deck, we watched the female dog lead Daq all around the edges of the stunning property. It seemed that she was instructing her new male friend how to help her protect her home.

When we headed back to the vehicle an hour later, the two dogs were resting comfortably in the shade, side by side.

There was no reason for sad goodbyes. We all realized that Daq had been blessed with an incredible new home. We chatted cheerfully all the way back, completely enthused with how this had turned out. We had not expected, when we prayed for help, that God would not only provide a new home for Daq but also would give him a highly skilled owner and a female partner to be at his side. It turned into a dog love story we could never have imagined.

We later heard that this magnificent pair led to many litters of adorable Great Pyrenees puppies.

YOUR STORY:
Cherished Pets

THINKING BACK

- Has an animal or pet of some kind played a significant role in your life?
- Did you choose this pet or did it seem to choose you?

THINKING INWARD

- How or why did this pet become important to you? How were emotional attachments or bonds with the pet created?
- Have you experienced sadness over the loss of a cherished pet? Has this loss impacted how you view other pet relationships?

THINKING OUTWARD

- Pet relationships mean so much to some people, yet others are not interested in pets. Have you noticed personality characteristics of the two different types of people?
- Have you connected with other people who have strong connections with their pets? What common traits do you share?

THINKING FORWARD

- What is your favourite memory of a cherished pet? Have you found a way to continue honouring this special animal in your life?
- Do you have any desires for your pets of the future?

Write a Prayer: Tell God every question, concern, or desire you have about the pets in your life.

Dear Heavenly Father,

You have created every living creature. You have blessed us with animals that provide us with companionship, loyalty, and protection. You care about each of the animals in our lives. I pray for every reader who might be mourning the loss of a special pet. Comfort them and ease their grief. I also pray for readers who have a need regarding their pet. I pray that You will help them find a solution for this need. And I also pray, dear Lord, for readers who do not have a special animal in their lives but desire companionship. You have an abundant supply and means of providing for our desires, Lord, and so I bring these requests before You.

In Your name, amen.

"Do not be anxious about anything, but in every situation, by prayer and petition, with thanksgiving, present your requests to God."

PHILIPPIANS 4:6

CHAPTER 16

Anxious

July 13, 2003, was a surreal day for our family. A massive moving truck roared into our farmyard that morning, and we realized there was no turning back. This move to a whole new life was going to happen, ready or not.

The movers began to load our belongings, strategically packing all of our furniture and our boxes. They had to fill every crevice so that nothing could shift as the truck travelled across the prairies and through the mountains, all the way to the coast of BC. We guided the movers to the best of our ability, trying to ignore the knots in our stomachs.

Leaving our cherished home on the farm was only one of the traumas we faced that day. The purchase of our house in Ladner appeared to have gone smoothly, but the paperwork had not yet been finalized. There was nothing more we could do except hope that it would all be completed.

By late afternoon, the moving truck was loaded to the brim. It rumbled out of our yard and headed off on the long journey. We would arrive at our home in Ladner many days before the big truck would get there. Even though we were already physically exhausted, we faced the task of loading up our smaller personal belongings into Kim's truck and trailer and my little SUV.

Adding to the physical and emotional toil of that day was the dreaded scene of saying our final goodbyes to Kim's family. There had been very little conversation about this major move with Kim's mom and dad or his sister and brother-in-law who lived nearby. It seemed they avoided the topic in hopes that our plans would change and the threat of us leaving would just go away. Much to their deep sadness, the moving day arrived, and goodbyes had to be spoken. There were tears, sobbing, and clinging hugs as we said the most difficult goodbyes imaginable.

Kim's head hung low and his shoulders drooped even lower as he drove out of his dad's yard with Kolby beside him in the black Chev truck pulling the trailer. Leaving his family was more difficult than he had imagined. If cancelling the move had still been possible, I'm sure he would have done it. I followed behind the trailer in my Hyundai SUV with Kraymer beside me. My back throbbed with aching pain from the many days of packing and moving boxes.

How in the world am I going to manage an 18-hour drive to BC in this condition?

I forced myself to think about the new life ahead of us. I clung with every morsel of faith I could muster to the belief that this move was truly God's plan for our family. I prayed for Kim's emotional state and for my body to have the strength and stamina to complete this trip.

Our little convoy made it as far as Medicine Hat, Alberta, then stopped at a motel for the night. I looked bad and felt even worse as I hobbled through the motel lobby, hunched over from the pain in my back. I didn't realize what a frightful sight I was until the motel clerk asked Kim if his mother would be all right. It was not a proud moment for Kim as he had to admit that it was his wife, not his mother, who had just shuffled past the front desk.

A bit more refreshed, we headed for BC early the next morning hoping to make it to Kelowna. We had friends there we could stay with, friends who had also made the move from Estevan, Saskatchewan, to BC. They would understand.

When we pulled into Kelowna, we were struck by the beauty of the Okanagan. I remember Kolby saying that we should have just moved there, it was so nice. Our friends opened their home for a bed and breakfast, and we were replenished physically and emotionally by their warmth and encouragement.

We were only four hours away from our destination now, but a new crisis emerged. The bank called with the devastating news that our loan to purchase the home in Ladner had not been approved. The actual house sale had not been finalized as we thought, due to a financial complication. We were no longer eligible for the keys to enter this special new home.

Did we pack our belongings and drive all this way with nowhere to go? If we can't get the money to buy this house, what will we do? How long will it take to find a different place? Where will we stay?

As we filled up our vehicles with gas before leaving Kelowna, we paused for a desperate prayer in the lot of the gas station.

Dear Lord, here we are in Kelowna on the way to our new home and a new life in Ladner. Not only do You see us, You are with us and You know about the bad news we got from our bank and why they cannot approve our loan to buy the house. Father, we do not know what to do. There is nothing we can do from Kelowna. We need Your help. Please guide the staff from the banks who are working on our loan issues. Please help this to go through so that we can get the keys for our house when we get there. We leave this in Your hands, Lord. Thank You for always caring about us and working on our behalf. Amen.

All we could do now was hope that God almighty would solve the problems with the banks while we continued on the last leg of the journey to our new life in Ladner.

Somewhere along the route from Kelowna to Delta, a miracle occurred. An excited bank employee called us with the wonderful news that the loan for the house purchase was approved. We weren't even sure how it happened, but our financial crisis was averted. As soon as we arrived, we would be able to open the front door and enter knowing that the home was ours.

Thank You, almighty God, for the paperwork miracle You performed!

Later, as I shared the physical and emotional difficulties of our move to BC with my oldest sister, she seemed to understand the magnitude of this life change for us. She described it as "jumping over the moon," and she couldn't have been more accurate.

YOUR STORY:

Concerns over Finances

THINKING BACK

- Have you ever made a life-changing decision, then second-guessed your choice and reconsidered what you were about to do?
- What caused you to keep moving forward or to change your mind?

THINKING INWARD

- What fears or emotional concerns have you experienced regarding finances?
- As you look back, were your fears valid? Have your experiences affected your concerns over money today?

THINKING OUTWARD

- What role did family members or loved ones have in your financial concerns?
- Was there a financial specialist working on your behalf? How did they advise or help you?

THINKING FORWARD

- If you were guiding or counselling someone who was facing a challenge similar to your experience, what would you say to them?
- Are you concerned about financial decisions that you will have to face in your future?

Write a Prayer: Tell God your every question, concern, and fear over finances in your life. Leave your burden with Him, and trust that He will guide you.

Dear Heavenly Father,

You are fully aware of the financial challenges and concerns over money that continue to plague us in this life. Your word says that the "love of money is a root of all kinds of evil" (1 Timothy 6:10) and we must guard against allowing money to become our priority. Yet, as You know, Lord, we need money to survive. We are in desperate need of Your guidance, Your wisdom, and Your help, dear Lord, in all matters of finances. I lift up to You now every reader who is experiencing stress over money issues. I pray that You will comfort them and help them deal effectively with the financial dilemma.

In Your name, amen.

"Be strong and courageous. Do not be afraid or terrified because of them, for the LORD your God goes with you; he will never leave you nor forsake you."

DEUTERONOMY 31:6

CHAPTER 17

Grateful

It was hard to keep from speeding as we got closer to our new home and our new lives in Ladner, BC. As we rounded the corner onto the street of our new address, we were bubbling with a mix of excited yet apprehensive feelings.

Kensington Place was a double cul-de-sac, so there was no traffic going by our home. The hum of Highway #10, however, was not far away. This was a sound that would take some getting used to. There was a little park with tennis courts directly behind our small yard, with agricultural land next to it. Cattle were grazing in a field only two blocks from our home. It was a bit of the familiar surrounded by a completely unfamiliar environment for this family of four from a farm in Saskatchewan.

We set up camp in our new home with our lawn chairs and blow-up mattresses. It would be several days before the arrival of our furniture and kitchen supplies. We improvised with paper plates and plastic silverware, enjoying the simple life with no major unpacking to do for a few days.

Our previous time spent in BC had been on holidays, so we all felt like we were on a grand holiday. Life in Ladner offered new treats that we didn't have on the farm, like riding bikes on pavement, playing tennis whenever we wanted to, walking to McDonald's for ice cream, and just relaxing in our backyard hot tub. We loved picking the wild blackberries that grew behind our house and trying to catch the wild bunnies that hopped in and out of our backyard. It was the middle of July, so we didn't have to worry about school or hockey or jobs, yet.

A weird cloud of marital complications floated into our home some days, threatening to steal my joy. I prayed it away, continually thanking and praising God for His protection and blessings on us. Kim and I didn't talk much about our issues; we pushed them aside. During one brief confrontation, Kim agreed that some counselling sessions might be helpful. We'd face that in the fall. For now, we just wanted to savour our first summer in BC.

There was plenty to worry about if I allowed my mind to go there. *How will the boys manage in their new school? Will they be able to make new friends who will be a good influence? Will they miss the farm, or will they be able to settle into this new life in the city?* I hoped with all of my heart that both of my boys would find a way to feel at home in their new worlds.

But this was not the time for worry or bringing those requests to God. This was the time to enjoy the blessings He had bestowed on us. I wanted to express my deep gratitude and honour God for all He had brought us through.

Dear Heavenly Father, words are just not adequate to fully thank You for all that You have done for us. Here we are in our new home in BC, Lord, with so many tough decisions and difficult times behind us. Your leading has been so clear, and Your protection, blessings, and guidance have been bountiful. You have fully supplied all of our needs according to Your riches (Philippians 4:19). We give You all the praise, honour, and glory for the countless answers to prayer. May we honour you in all we do and bring glory to Your name as we live our lives for You in BC. Amen.

We spent many summer days exploring the area and enjoying a staycation in our new province. We were fascinated with the different plants and trees that grew in the coastal BC climate. Just beyond the agricultural land behind our home was a nursery that sold some of the unique bushes and trees that would not have survived the harsh winters of Saskatchewan. Kraymer noticed that they sold palm trees and that other yards in the area had some, which were tall and thriving. He decided we should have palm trees in our yard too.

Before we could stop him, he set off on foot with a wheelbarrow and a pocket full of his earnings from lawn mowing in search of new trees for our yard. He had that fresh-off-the-farm look as he pushed the wheelbarrow containing a newly purchased palm tree down the sidewalk that led back to our house. He had enough money for two, so eventually we had two freshly planted palm trees next to our hot tub in the backyard. He named them George and Newman from his favourite show, *Seinfeld*.

We enjoyed our neighbourhood and quickly got to know the families living on our street. We had no idea when we purchased this home on Kensington Place that we were joining a group of long-time closely knit neighbours. Most of the families on the cul-de-sac had lived there for many, many years. They knew each other well and celebrated Christmas, Easter, and Halloween together, taking turns planning events on the street that everyone could enjoy.

The family that had previously lived in our home had been very closely connected to everyone in the neighbourhood. Sadly, a year and a half before they sold to us, they suffered the tragic loss of their teenage son in a devastating car accident. The horrific crash had involved other youth from Ladner, causing further devastation and controversy in the community. The Kensington Place neighbourhood had mourned deeply with the previous owners of our home over the loss of their oldest son. Neighbourhood gatherings had been toned down out of respect for this family.

Despite very close ties, selling the home was a step forward for the mourning family, who were trying to put their painful past behind them by moving to a new house in a different neighbourhood. It seemed the arrival of our family to the cul-de-sac allowed the Kensington Place neighbourhood a chance to move forward as well and live a bit more joyfully again.

All of the neighbours greeted us warmly and invited us into the neighbourhood celebrations right from the start. Our neighbours to the left welcomed us with their wonderful sense of humour and became dear friends from day one. They hosted the first special event to be celebrated together—Halloween. Joining with the neighbours, we experienced the fun and craziness of fireworks and firecrackers, a very different kind of Halloween than we had experienced in Saskatchewan. During Christmas, our neighbours to the right hosted a special holiday brunch, and at Easter we all took part in the neighbourhood Easter egg hunt.

When we moved so far from home, we knew that special occasions might bring feelings of deep loneliness. We had no idea we would have such a friendly neighbourhood and meet people that would warmly welcome us into their lives.

God knew all about this street long before we got here.

It was hard to even imagine that less than a year before we were sitting at our kitchen table on our farm in Saskatchewan looking at a map of the lower mainland and wondering where we should go. We looked at many subdivisions and hundreds of streets. It was surreal now to realize how God had not only led us to our new home, He led us to this street and this unique and special neighbourhood.

How could we ever thank God enough for His answers to those prayers back in Saskatchewan?

YOUR STORY:
Gratitude

THINKING BACK
- Can you recall a time in your life when you felt great satisfaction, fully realizing that you were experiencing your heart's desire?
- Was this an expected blessing or a complete surprise? What were some of the details that led to your contentment?

THINKING INWARD
- Were there worries or threats that tried to rob you of the joy or the satisfaction of the blessing? If so, how did you deal with the "joy robbers"?
- How did you celebrate or express thanksgiving for this time or place of blessing?

THINKING OUTWARD
- Did family members or friends notice the blessings that you were experiencing? How did they react?
- Did your blessing cause a "ripple effect" and bless other people around you (i.e. your neighbourhood or your work world)?

THINKING FORWARD
- Have you developed a habit of gratitude to help you recount your blessings every day, so they don't go unnoticed?
- How have your seasons of thanksgiving affected your view of the place you are in today and what you might face in the future?

Write a Prayer: Share a prayer of thanksgiving with God for every gift or blessing you are enjoying today.

Dear Heavenly Father,

Your word states in Ecclesiastes that "There is a time for everything, and a season for every activity under the heavens … a time to weep and a time to laugh, a time to mourn and a time to dance" (3:1, 4). I want to thank You, Lord, for the seasons of blessing, when we can relax, enjoy life, and relish the goodness of Your gifts to us. I lift up readers to You now, Lord, who are living in a time of laughter and dancing, and I pray that they would realize the source of their blessings and offer up praise and thanksgiving to You. I also lift up readers who are living in a time of weeping and mourning. Help them to see that this season will come to an end, and a time of being joyful will come again.

In Your name, amen.

"I will give thanks to you LORD, with all my heart;
I will tell of all your wonderful deeds."

PSALM 9:1

CHAPTER 18
Discouraged

The lazy, hazy bliss of our first summer in BC passed all too quickly. Before the weather began to show signs of cooling, we noticed the dreaded back-to-school advertisements on TV, forcing us to think about what lay ahead. As we neared the end of August, we had to face the reality of a new school, new jobs, and more unavoidable life adjustments.

The boys were starting grades eight and eleven at Delta Secondary School in Ladner—a school with more than two thousand students, grades eight to twelve. They had a few new friends from the neighbourhood and their hockey tryouts but really had no idea what to expect at their new school. *What will teachers and classes be like in this huge new school? How will they find their place in this mass of kids from Delta?*

Kolby faced the first day bravely, relying on his outgoing personality and upbeat attitude, as usual. He was confident that he would have no problem making new friends. Kraymer didn't have that same confidence, but he had already earned a goalie position on the AAA Bantam Delta Storm hockey team. One of the boys on his new hockey team would be in his classes. Despite their bravery, I could see and feel every bit of their nervousness as they headed to their first day of school at DSS.

Kraymer adjusted to the new school better than expected. His "hot-new-goalie-in-town" status earned him some instant friends. But Kolby's expectations about how things would roll out in the new school turned out to be deeply disappointing. He came home with less enthusiasm every day.

About a week after school started, the boys forgot their lunch, and I had to bring it to them at school. As I pulled up to the area near the front entry, my heart leaped, then sank to the pit of my stomach. There Kraymer sat on the lawn, joking around with his new buddies, looking like he belonged. Kolby sat there too, alone. He looked like an awkward tagalong to his little brother's gang. No grade eleven student wants to be seen hanging out with a group of grade-eighters. How humiliating.

It was a disheartening sight, but it confirmed our fears about what was actually happening in Kolby's world at this new school. Most grade eleven students have been together since grade eight and have well established friends and cliques. Despite the friendliness of a newcomer, cracking into a clique was difficult. Kolby's positive outlook deflated a bit more every day as he came home with no mention of a successful friend connection.

To make matters worse, Kolby's first choice for playing hockey that season was the Delta Ice Hawks. He tried out for the junior B team with full confidence that he had the skill to make it. The day he was cut from the team, he hit rock bottom. With no hockey team and no friends, Kolby's optimistic view of his new life in BC faded to black. We wanted to cheer him up and pull him out of his blues, but our oldest son barricaded himself in his room, trying to hide from the cruelty of life. Kim and I couldn't help but blame ourselves for taking our boy away from his familiar and secure environment back in Saskatchewan where his life made sense.

I shared my regret and my fears tearfully to God in prayer, asking Him to help our boys to fully adjust and especially for Kolby to find his unique place in this new world. Kim also needed prayer, and so did I. Neither of us had found the work we had hoped for. Three of us in the family were losing our optimistic view of life in BC, our spirits sinking a bit lower each day.

Dear Lord, how badly we need You, Your help, Your comfort, and Your guidance. Your word says that You are always with us, that You never leave us nor forsake us (Hebrews 13:5), and that we are to cast our cares upon You and You will sustain us (Psalm 55:22). Lord, I want to cast Kolby's burdens on You today. You know even more fully than I do just how discouraged he is about his new life here. You know and understand the depth of his disappointments and the sadness he feels today. I ask, dear Lord, that You surround him with Your love and encourage him somehow. Help him to see that this, too, shall pass and that his life will get better. Carry him through this valley, I pray. I leave him in Your hands today.

And Father, I ask the same for Kim and for me. We are both discouraged about our lack of desired work. Please guide us, I pray, dear Lord, and help us to hold on to You and Your promises. I know You are with us, Lord. Amen.

An unexpected visitor showed up at our home that week. It was the trainer of the Vancouver Giants team. He had heard about Kolby being cut from the Ice Hawks and somehow understood how hard this was for our son. The trainer brought his unique sense of humour to our home, but he also came with a gift for Kolby. It was the movie *Rudy*, the story of a football player who overcame immense odds to achieve his football dreams. It was the trainer's contagious sense of humour that got Kolby out his room and laughing a little again, and the motivational story of the movie continued the healing process as our son watched it many times.

By the month of November, our family routines became a bit more normal as we settled into a weekly schedule of school and hockey practices. Kolby's ability to persevere emerged again, and he mustered up the courage to try out for a second-choice hockey team. He was successful at earning a position on the Delta Midget AAA team and started to regain his life optimism.

It took a few months, but Kolby finally connected with a few classmates and slid into a clique at school made up of an eclectic group of guys who were not all hockey players but were talented athletes. Their love of sports was their common connector, so Kolby fit right in. He no longer had to eat lunch alone, since he was often invited to a friend's house right across the street from the school.

Thank You, dear Lord, for lifting our son out of despair and leading him to a new and different path.

Kim had started working with the Vancouver Giants hockey team, but his role was not well defined. He continued to scout for players in the lower mainland, as he had done in Saskatchewan, and he did some work in the area of player development, but the specific role that he was hoping for was not materializing. Even if he had jumped into a well-defined position, it was obvious that working with the WHL was not going to pay well enough for the cost of living in BC.

Kim had always supplemented our farm income with house building and renovation work in Saskatchewan. It was obvious that he was going to have to start looking for construction or renovation jobs to help pay the bills in BC. Fortunately, he was skilled in almost all areas of building, from house framing to tile laying. He dreaded the thought of taking a "lunch-pail" job, as he described it, but he soon found himself working on a seniors' residence building project in Ladner. It was not how he wanted to spend his time in BC, but it did allow him to keep working closely with the hockey team. It would help pay the bills, for now.

Our marriage issues took a back seat, once again, to our concerns for the boys and financial matters. But we had decided months earlier to see a counsellor, so we booked an appointment with a reputable marriage specialist in Surrey. The drive to Surrey was awkward with silence. What we really needed was an "honesty session," where our true and hidden feelings could be expressed, but we were both too guarded to start that conversation. The counsellor tried his best to open the communication and get to the heart of the matter. Neither of us knew how to articulate our struggles.

On the way home we agreed that the session was useless. It seemed to both of us that he misunderstood our personalities and didn't have any helpful guidance to offer. We never went back.

The only accomplishment of that one visit might have been our willingness to go. It reaffirmed our commitment to each other.

Continue guiding and helping us, I pray, Lord. I know You are with us.

The heaviness of disappointments that fall lightened as both boys became more settled and our marriage issues were no longer being ignored. It was time now to focus on jobs and find ways to increase our earning potential in this new province.

YOUR STORY:

Disappointment

THINKING BACK

- Have you ever had high hopes or expectations about something coming in your future but then had to face deep disappointment about how it turned out?
- What was the cause(s) of your disappointment?

THINKING INWARD

- How did the disappointment affect your mental health overall? How did you deal with this disappointment?
- What brought relief or helped to lift your spirits?

THINKING OUTWARD

- Were there any small comforts or "dream supporters" that came into your life at the time to help you deal with the disappointment?
- Did you sense God's presence in your life giving you some hope and helping you to persevere?

THINKING FORWARD

- Has this past disappointment affected the amount of hope and expectation you feel about upcoming events or plans in your future?
- Is there a disappointment in your life today that you would like to bring to God in prayer?

Write a Prayer: Share with God the deepest disappointments that you are experiencing in your life. Ask Him for encouragement and strength to move forward.

Dear Heavenly Father,

You have stated, "in this world you will have trouble" (John 16:33). This statement, unfortunately, is true. Trouble in this life is unavoidable, and times of discouragement are common to everyone. Dealing with disappointment is not easy, and it is hard to find encouragement in the midst of a dark time. But You have also said, "Take heart! I have overcome the world" (John 16:33). Help us, I pray, to look to You and be encouraged. Help us to place our hope and trust in You and cast our discouragement at Your feet. Your word promises that our God will "restore you and make you strong, firm and steadfast" (1 Peter 5:10). We ask for this today.

In Your name, amen.

"Why, my soul, are you downcast?
Why so disturbed within me?
Put your hope in God, for I will yet praise him,
my Savior and my God."

PSALM 42:11

CHAPTER 19

Impatient

The amount of cover letters I had created for job applications was adding up to a monumental number in my computer files. The number of responses from these applications, however, was far from impressive. That number was zero.

Why are my applications ignored? Why can I not even get shortlisted for an interview?

I was beginning to realize that I would not be able to jump into the type of contract work that I had done in Saskatchewan. I was living the sad truth that it's not what you know but who you know that opens the door to an organization. I did not have the necessary network in BC to find the work or to verify my ability to do the work. What I had accomplished outside of Vancouver was not creditable in the Vancouver job market without some personal connections.

Even though it was my last choice, I applied to do substitute teaching work or TOC (teacher on call) work in Delta as a backup plan. A few calls started to come for me in October. I accepted the first few opportunities naively, but soon realized I needed more knowledge of these school systems and more preparation for the unexpected duties that were thrown at me. I screened the calls a bit more and tried to accept the jobs that were a better fit with my teaching background and experiences, but I soon had to admit the sad truth. I hated TOC work.

Everything I used to appreciate about teaching didn't happen in the TOC world. I was an expert in creating interesting lesson plans, but as a TOC, you simply have to give the students whatever work their absent teacher had planned for them, which was usually boring busy work. My other favourite part of teaching was building relationships with students. As a TOC, I didn't even have the chance to learn the students' names. Most of the time, the students didn't care what my name was, and some school staffs actually referred to me by my TOC number instead of my name. No one noticed or cared that I had 16 years of teaching experience or that I had written curriculum and trained other teachers. I was back to the absolute bottom of the teaching ladder. It was humiliating to the core.

On one of the better TOC jobs, I spotted a notice on the teachers' bulletin board about an upcoming career education conference taking place in Vancouver. One of the key themes of this conference was portfolios and how to implement them with secondary school students. Before leaving Saskatchewan, I had conducted many workshops on career portfolios for teachers and employment counsellors, so this conference theme was dead centre in my area of expertise. I registered that evening; I could hardly wait to attend. It felt like God had led me to find out about this conference, and my hopes began to rise again.

The day finally arrived, and I found my way to Hastings Street, downtown Vancouver, for the conference. I was enthralled with every one of the morning sessions I attended and felt like my former professional self, amidst a group of like-minded educators with similar interests.

During the lunch session, I found myself sitting next to a woman who had previously resided in Estevan, Saskatchewan. She knew many of my colleagues from Estevan Jr. High. She was now living in Victoria, working for Open School BC. The friendly woman at my lunch table was genuinely interested in my knowledge of portfolios and told me about some contract work that was coming up soon, writing content about portfolios for a new distance education course. This sounded like it could be my first big break. I made sure to do all the follow-up and sent in my very best application for this possible contract work with Open School BC.

As the weeks and months passed by with no contract offers coming my way, I doubted myself and my previous confidence.

Did I raise my hopes in vain? Did I overestimate God's leading at the November conference?

I brought my confusion and frustration to God in prayer.

Dear Lord, I praise You and thank You for every time You have led and guided me in past career paths and decisions. As You know, I trust in You and believe in the awesome promise You gave to us in Psalm 32:8. You said, "I will instruct and teach you in the way you should go; I will counsel you with my loving eye on you."

I really thought You guided me to that conference in November, Lord. It seemed like too much of an uncanny coincidence that I sat beside a woman from Estevan at lunch, a former teacher from Saskatchewan. You know the goose bumps I had, Lord, when she told me about the upcoming work for someone with knowledge of portfolios.

But the silence is killing me, Lord. Why haven't I heard from her? Did I misunderstand Your guidance? If this was not from You, Lord, please help me to forget about it and find another lead. Or, if it really was from You, help me to be patient, Lord. I love You, Lord, and I really do want to trust You in all things. Amen.

It took until February, but I finally got the reply from Victoria that I was hoping and praying for. I was offered the contract position with Open School BC that the woman from Estevan had told me about at the conference.

I was grinning from ear to ear as I took my first ferry trip to Victoria for orientation with Open School BC to learn more about the new course that I would be working on. I was able to block my name from the TOC list for the rest of that year.

Hurrah, hurrah! No more TOC work! Happy dance!

I was going to work in my little home office in our Ladner house, writing modules for the grade ten distance education course.

Unfortunately, not everyone in our family was grinning or doing a happy dance. Kim was not enjoying his "lunch-pail" job at the Ladner Senior Residence and was less than thrilled with the pay he was earning at both of his jobs. His prayers had not yet been answered.

As I continued praying for my husband, I wasn't sure what to ask for. Just bringing my concerns to God brought some unexplainable comfort. I realized, more fully now, that praying is not always about asking God for something but is sometimes simply coming alongside of Him, recognizing that He is at work behind the scenes in ways we cannot see.

YOUR STORY:

A Time of Waiting

THINKING BACK

- Have you ever waited impatiently for a response from God that just wasn't coming? As you look back, can you identify reasons why the answer took so long?
- How did you manage your period of waiting?

THINKING INWARD

- What were the self-doubts that you had to battle during this time?
- Did self-questioning or loss of trust in your beliefs become an added challenge? How did you deal with this?

THINKING OUTWARD

- Did you share your doubts with anyone? Did they help you see possible reasons for the delay?
- What is the best way to encourage someone who is in this period of waiting?

THINKING FORWARD

- What have your past experiences of waiting taught you about patience or trust regarding future events that might require you to wait?
- Are you still waiting for a response or something from God that you have prayed about for a long time?

Write a Prayer: Share your concern over a lack of response from God with Him again. Ask Him to help you to continue trusting and believing that He is at work behind the scenes of your life.

Dear Heavenly Father,

Time passes so slowly for us some days. It is easy to become anxious and frustrated when something takes much longer than we expect. But You see ahead of us, dear Lord, and You know the best timing and outcome of every situation. I lift up to You every reader who is anxiously waiting for something. I pray that You would give them patience. Help them to see why a "yellow light" remains and to trust in You regarding the timing of what they hope for and are asking for. Be near to them, I pray, and help them to see that You have not abandoned them. You will answer in Your time and in Your perfect way.

In Your name, amen.

"Those who hope in the LORD will renew their strength.

They will soar on wings like eagles;

they will run and not be weary,

they will walk and not be faint."

ISAIAH 40:31

CHAPTER 20

Hoping

By the summer of 2004, one year after we arrived in BC, we felt quite firmly planted in our lives in Ladner. Money was still an issue, but moving back to Saskatchewan was not even on our radar. We didn't even discuss the idea of returning to our former lives.

We focused more on how we could access additional funds for the high costs of living in BC. We put our Saskatchewan farm up for sale and started to liquidate other assets to help pay our bills. It was a temporary solution until we both found better paying, more permanent work.

Feeling more rooted in our new home, we decided the timing might be right for another family member. We missed our precious Great Pyrenees dog, Daq, and we longed for a family pet once again. Both boys were playing ball that summer, and we envied the families that came to the ballpark with their family pets.

One dog in particular caught my eye. He was a soft-coated wheaten terrier that looked like a stuffed animal and felt like one too. I asked around and scoured websites where these unique dogs could be purchased.

We found a well-respected breeder in Langley called Designer Dogs who bred wheaten terriers with poodles and other breeds. Her dogs were in high demand, so in order to get on the wait list, our family had to submit a letter describing why we would make good dog owners. We were told that it would take till the fall or later before our names would arrive near the top of the list. I was deeply disappointed it would take so long. We wanted to have the dog for the summer while the boys were on holidays. We committed our hopes for a new dog to God in prayer, knowing that His timing is always perfect.

Dear Lord, we can't help but recall the incredible way that You answered our prayers for Daq. You heard our plea for a new home for Daq, and You provided an awesome place for him. We think we are ready now for a new dog to join our family, and summer would be the best time. This seems like a trivial need to bother You with, but You already know how we feel. We are so disappointed to think we might have to wait for the fall or even later. I want to leave this in Your hands, Lord, and trust in Your perfect timing. I also trust that You will help us find the dog that is the right one for us. I ask this in Your name, Lord. Amen.

It was in July, shortly after the anniversary of our first year in BC, when we got an unexpected call from the breeder in Langley. The family at the top of the list had decided to delay getting their dog. Even though we were way down the list, the breeder had read our letter and chosen our family for the dog that was now available.

You are so amazing, God! I can hardly believe this answer to prayer. You moved us to the top of the list, just like that.

We could hardly contain our excitement as we drove to Langley to claim our new puppy. When we arrived at the breeder's acreage, we could see several litters of hyperactive but adorable puppies scampering around their enclosed area. We watched them with delight, wondering which one was going to be ours. The breeder came over and started to call the puppies by name. All of the dogs were spoken for and had already been named by their future families. Then she pointed out one male puppy hiding under a little bridge at the back of their play area. As she reached under the bridge calling him to come, the shy pup timidly crawled towards her. This was our dog. One of his parents had been a soft-coated wheaten terrier; the other parent was a schnoodle, a cross between a poodle and a schnauzer.

It was love at first sight for all of us. He had fluffy apricot-coloured fur and warm brown eyes that seemed more like a person's than a dog's.

We cuddled our new puppy all the way home, discussing what name suited him best. We just couldn't decide. As we watched a football game on TV later that day, Kim commented that our puppy's fur kind of resembled the hair of the BC Lions' coach Wally Buono. This was the perfect name—Wally. It was complicated to describe his actual breed, so we just referred to him as Wally the Woodle. We had no idea what a priceless family member Wally would become.

Kim accepted a job that summer redoing the roof on the house of one of the Vancouver Giants' coaches. He decided this would be a good summer job for both of our boys, so shortly after we got Wally the three of them ventured off for long days of work. This left me to do the puppy training. I spent all day with Wally and did my best to train him and teach him the basic commands of sit, lie down, and shake a paw. Wally and I bonded that summer, and I have often wondered if this is why Wally is more attached to me than to any other family member.

Wally grew to be more the size of a poodle than a wheaten terrier, but along with his size came a huge character and a gentle, easygoing personality. He did have a few bouts of bad behaviour, as one paper boy in Delta could verify, but for the most part Wally has been an undeniably excellent pet for our family. We have often marvelled at his human-like qualities and his intuitive understanding of what we are saying to him.

YOUR STORY:

Coincidences

THINKING BACK

- Can you recall small concerns, needs, or hopes that have troubled you over a period of time? What happened to these concerns?
- When hopes and prayers are answered quickly, the result may seem like a coincidence. Can you identify a "coincidence" like this in your life?

THINKING INWARD

- What emotions did you experience with this "small but mighty" coincidence in your life?
- Did you allow yourself to feel joyful over this blessing, or did it seem too insignificant or fleeting to celebrate?

THINKING OUTWARD

- Did you share your blessing with any family, friends, or co-workers? How did they react?
- Have you ever noticed a comment about a coincidence in someone else's life? What was your belief about their story of coincidence?

THINKING FORWARD

- Have past coincidences affected how you view your hopes and desires for the future?
- Do you have a prayer request that you would like to bring to God about something you are hoping for that seems insignificant but is still important to you?

Write a Prayer: Create a list for God of things that concern you every day but might seem too small to bring to Him in prayer.

Dear Heavenly Father,

It often feels like some of our hopes are not important enough to pray about. We don't want to bother You with the small requests. But You know us, Father; You know the number of hairs on our head (Luke 12:7), and You know all about these smaller desires that are significant in our minds. I lift up to You now, Lord, any request that seems too small for readers to bring to You. I ask that You act on their behalf and help them with these desires. Your timing is perfect, Lord, and we thank You for every quick response when that is Your plan. Help us to not overlook the answer to our prayers, calling it "coincidence." May we recognize that You are the giver of all good gifts.

In Your name, amen.

"Every good and perfect gift is from above, coming down from the Father of the heavenly lights, who does not change like shifting shadows."

JAMES 1:17

CHAPTER 21

Infuriated

New province, new city, new schools, new jobs, new home, and new neighbours: our family had endured enough change in the past year to last a lifetime. But our second fall in BC brought the threat of more changes that made me uncomfortable from the first mention of the idea.

Kim's frustrations with small renovation jobs were draining him. He began to look for bigger projects. His entrepreneurial thinking led him to the idea that if he could find a house that had good value but needed a full renovation, he could do all the work and make a substantial profit. The Vancouver housing market held great promise for this kind of investment.

He showed me a few houses that he thought had potential, but I was not the slightest bit interested in his idea. I could not imagine how we would make it work financially. The last thing I wanted to do was sell our beloved home in Ladner and leave our special neighbourhood. But Kim couldn't let go of his idea.

Another change taking place involved the boys' schooling. The Vancouver Giants team had partnered with Delta School District to start a hockey academy at South Delta Secondary School in Tsawwassen. Kraymer was just the right age and fit the desired profile of a student for this academy. If he attended, it would involve a change in schools for him, which meant that our two boys would be attending different schools. These possible changes hung like threatening storm clouds over our heads.

As we considered the pros and the cons of the hockey academy in Tsawwassen, the pros seemed to outweigh the cons. Others told us that this was a rare opportunity for Kraymer. An announcement about a change in Kim's role with the hockey team tipped us in favour of enrolling Kraymer in the academy. One of Kim's new duties was going to include on-ice instruction for the academy every morning. This meant that Kraymer could ride with his dad to school and have him nearby for the first part of his day in this new environment.

Okay. I think I can handle this change in schools now. Thank You, God, for making this all right. Now, if only this house threat would go away.

As Kim spent more time in the community of Tsawwassen, he recognized the value of real estate in that area. In the summer, he spotted a house for sale that had a "framed" view of the ocean from the front patio. It was on a street with high-end homes that had received major renovations due to the location and view. But the house that Kim had his eye on was in its original state. Not a single update or renovation had been done to it. The owners had lived there for 30 years and were planning to move to a seniors' residence.

Kim convinced me to take a look at the Tsawwassen house with "huge potential," despite my lack of interest. He had been thinking about the house for several months and just couldn't get it out of his head. He was surprised it was still on the market.

Driving up to the front of the house was encouraging despite the lack of care it had received. It held stately curb appeal with red brick and white shutters on the front and majestic white pillars framing the front entry. The interior, however, was a disaster. The kitchen was tiny, dark, and filthy. A dysfunctional laundry room, right next to the kitchen, stole space from the living room at the front of the house. The bedrooms were all small with tiny, impractical closets. The bathrooms were outdated with disgusting stains from long-term use. A putrid aroma engulfed the entire house. I could hardly wait to get out of there. The mere thought of buying that house made my stomach retch.

Move into that house? You have got to be kidding!

My eyes saw a disgusting, smelly old house. Kim's eyes saw a diamond in the rough, a house with huge potential for increasing financial equity. His visionary mind had already created a new floor plan that would transform the home to the level of grandeur of other homes on the street. Kim insisted this was an excellent financial opportunity. I was against the idea with every fibre of my being.

How can he think about uprooting our family again?!

Angry and bitter words shot back and forth. Kim accused me of holding up a chance for financial progress. I couldn't believe he would even consider the idea of buying this horrid house, forcing our family to move again. Our opposing points of view spurred each other with hurtful accusations that churned with rage. Past arguments were dredged up. Former hurts that were almost forgotten resurfaced and reopened painful wounds. When the fighting reached a peak that went nowhere, we settled into our familiar pattern of "I'm right, you're wrong" stubborn silence.

I couldn't even bring myself to pray about this house. I just prayed for our marriage and that we could quit fighting and stop hurting each other.

Dear Lord, I praise You and thank You for all things. Even though I don't feel like it today, I thank You for my husband. You have blessed me with a skilled and ambitious partner. But as You know, Lord, sometimes his ideas just don't make sense in my mind. Father, I pray that, somehow, You would help us get through the painful place we are in right now. We just can't agree. Guide us both, I pray, and help us to stop fighting. You have helped us with this many times before, Lord, and so I ask again, please restore peace to our marriage. I ask this in Your name, Lord. Amen.

After more heated arguments, followed by spells of painful silence, we finally called a truce. The feelings of anger and resentment were exhausting for both of us. We forced ourselves to talk again, trying to communicate without anger in an "honesty session." We needed to get to the heart of the deep feelings behind our strong opinions. Each of us expressed what was most important to us and why we felt that way. We arrived at a difficult compromise.

Kim came up with a plan that would possibly allow us to go ahead with the renovation project without having to sell our Ladner house. I consented to looking into the financial possibility of his idea. If the bank would grant us the money, Kim would renovate the house and revive it to a presentable state before we had to consider leaving our Ladner home.

We entered the bank with hesitation, Kim walking a few steps ahead of me. Kim nervously defended our request for a line of credit to buy and renovate the Tsawwassen house without selling our Ladner home first. It defied all logic and general guidelines for loaning money, but for some reason, the bank approved our request. We became the owners of two houses in Delta, with a mortgage and a line of credit.

Kim started work on the massive renovation by gutting most of the house to create the new floor plan. Walls were removed, creating a large open space kitchen and family room. The newly created family room had large patio doors that opened up to a view of the ocean where the ferries arrived at the Tsawwassen port. Bathrooms were refurbished, every piece replaced by shiny and new fixtures. A free-standing soaker tub and a specialty shower with rain head were installed in the newly created ensuite.

Kim's youngest sister and her husband came from Saskatchewan to help with the job of painting. With their help, the walls came alive with well-chosen colours. The full upper floor of the home became chic and modern. Fresh paint, new carpets, and an updated bathroom revived the lower level.

As the Tsawwassen house began to take shape, we put our beloved Ladner home up for sale. It did not take long to sell, and before our other house was fully ready, we packed up once again and moved, on April 27, 2005, only a few miles away this time, to Glenwood Drive, Tsawwassen. The kitchen and bathroom sinks weren't fully functioning yet, but we had a roof over our heads and a home that smelled fresh and new.

After our first night in the newly renovated house, I woke up with a renewed sense of peace, along with an unexpected sense of excitement. I had a new community to explore, and a short daily walk would lead me to a beach on the ocean.

I didn't expect it to turn out like this, God. Thank You for guiding us through this deep valley to the other side.

Peace and forgiveness returned to our marriage. Kim thrived on the renovation work and felt a huge sense of satisfaction with the accomplishments of his labour. He swelled with pride and renewed confidence in his abilities as visitors to our home marvelled at the extreme transformation. We were both proud of our new home and proud of each other as we reached a new level of teamwork in our marriage.

We did it. We had mastered yet another change. Another move and a difficult and hurtful season of arguments in our marriage were now in the rear-view mirror. It was time to relax and enjoy life a little.

YOUR STORY:

Dealing with Conflict

THINKING BACK

- Even though it might be painful to recall, think of a time when you experienced conflict in your life. What was the source of this conflict?
- What details of this conflict added to the level of difficulty that it caused in your life?

THINKING INWARD

- How did you manage the tension in your life during this conflict?
- Which of the solutions to resolving the conflict created the most angst for you? How did you begin moving towards a possible resolution?

THINKING OUTWARD

- Were you able to identify pros and cons of the possible solutions? Were any other methods used to help you see another perspective?
- Were family members, friends, or counsellors involved in the conflict? Did their opinions help or hinder the path to reaching a resolution?

THINKING FORWARD

- What have you learned about resolving conflict from your past that might help you in the future?
- Are you involved in a conflict today that needs prayer?

Write a Prayer: Tell God all about the conflict you are facing. Even though it is difficult, ask God to be with the person(s) causing the conflict in your life and ask for His guidance in reaching a peaceful resolution.

Dear Heavenly Father,

You see and You know that relationships are complicated. There are times we can't live without each other and times we can't live with each other. I pray for our relationships, dear Lord, and ask that You would protect and guide us in all aspects of our interactions with the people in our life. We need Your wisdom, Lord, to communicate and understand each other's point of view. Help us to deal with conflict effectively today, Lord. Lead us, I pray, to a resolution, and restore peace and love in our relationships.

In Your name, amen.

"Get rid of all bitterness, rage and anger ...

Be kind and compassionate to one another,

forgiving each other, just as in Christ God forgave you."

EPHESIANS 4:31–32

CHAPTER 22
Letting Go

Even though I felt a bit guilty, I splurged on a stylish new dress. I justified the price tag, telling the clerk that it was my son's graduation.

I haven't had a new dress for so long. I want to look my best for Kolby's big day.

I was so proud of Kolby and how well he had done in grade twelve despite all the changes he had endured. We invested in a classy pinstriped suit for him with a striking orange shirt and coordinating tie. He picked out some trendy new sunglasses to go with the ensemble, doing his very best to look the role of the cool, confident grad.

But on graduation day, I could see that he was just playing a role. He wasn't quite himself. It was obvious that the graduation celebration here in Delta was much different than he expected. We had both pictured the day to be more like it was in Estevan, Saskatchewan. Families were more involved there, and everyone came dressed to the nines. In Ladner, there were far too many grads to involve families. The entire event was more low-key for family members, who stood awkwardly at the back of the auditorium. Everyone, except grads, came to the event in everyday casual wear.

This dress was a waste of money. I am totally overdressed for this event.

From our disadvantaged place among the long rows of families, it was hard to even get a clear sighting of our son walking across the stage.

During the graduation festivities, I detected a hint of longing for Saskatchewan in Kolby that I hadn't seen in a while. I didn't realize how serious that hint would be when it came to a major decision he was mulling over in his mind.

As our third fall in BC was approaching, we were fully settled into our home in Tsawwassen with a shiny new and fully functioning kitchen and finished new bathrooms. Wally and I enjoyed our daily walk down the hill to the ocean and back. Kolby was looking into which courses to take at Kwantlen, a local college that would allow him to continue living at home. Kraymer would soon be starting grade ten at the hockey academy at South Delta Secondary School in Tsawwassen, which was now very close to our home. The school year ahead for both boys looked promising and "as it should be" in my mind, but Kolby's mind was in a different place.

For some reason, Kolby couldn't settle into the idea of attending Kwantlen College. His cousin in Saskatchewan, his best buddy from childhood, was going to attend Briercrest College in Caronport, Saskatchewan. He was going to take business courses and would be playing college-level hockey at Briercrest. This plan sounded alluring to Kolby. Along with the chance to take courses in business, he could live in the dorm next to his cousin and play on the same hockey team. He would have his dear auntie and uncle close by, like in the good old days.

The idea of Kolby going back to Saskatchewan did not appeal to us at all when he first mentioned it. One of the benefits of where we now lived was that Kolby had full access to several different universities and colleges while living at home. But that wasn't what he wanted. We all prayed about it, sincerely seeking God's guidance as to the best place for Kolby to be for his first year of college.

Dear Lord, we thank You for Your great wisdom and guidance and for Your perfect plan for our lives. Lord, we know that we are to trust You with all of our hearts and lean not on our own understanding. We want to submit to You and allow You to direct our paths. We lift Kolby up to You today, and we ask that You show him and us the best path for him to take. His desire to go back to Saskatchewan for college, Lord, is a very hard plan for us to accept. We would so much rather have him go to college here and stay with us. Please show us Your best path for him, Lord, and help us all to agree on this decision. We thank You, Lord, that we can trust You to lead Kolby in the direction that lines up with Your perfect plan for his life. Amen.

Just talking about going to college in Caronport made Kolby's eyes light up. We couldn't deny our son's reasons for wanting to go back to his home province, and we knew that Caronport would be a safe and positive environment for his first year away from home. So, despite our selfish preferences, we helped our eldest son pack up and let him go in the direction he desired, back to Saskatchewan.

The house was strangely quiet with only one boy at home. Kraymer and Kim left early in the morning for the hockey academy. Wally and I looked at each other, wondering what we should be doing. We wandered around the house and often found ourselves in Kolby's empty bedroom. The sadness was overwhelming some days, but every phone call with Kolby revealed how happy he was. He shared stories of crazy pranks happening in his dorm and the bonding rituals of his first college hockey team. His marks were good and proved that he was learning.

It was obvious that our eldest son was having the time of his life and fully enjoying his college experience at Briercrest. Letting go and letting God take the reins of our eldest son's life was a difficult step as parents, but we trusted that God would direct his path and guide him in all life choices.

YOUR STORY:

Separation

THINKING BACK
- Have you ever faced the hard choice of supporting a loved one's decision to move or travel far away from you?
- What factors did you have to consider before making the decision to support (or not support) your loved one's choices?

THINKING INWARD
- What part of "letting go" was the most challenging for you?
- How did you manage or cope with life during the difficult decision time period?

THINKING OUTWARD
- How did your loved one's choice impact your life or the lives of other family members?
- Were you able to see a positive outcome in their move away from you? How did you stay in touch or keep the communication going with your loved one?

THINKING FORWARD
- What have you learned from past experiences of letting go that will guide you in the future?
- Are you currently missing someone in your life who is no longer living close to you?

Write a Prayer: Share with God your deepest feelings about the person you are missing today. Give Him your sadness and ask Him to comfort the ache in your heart.

Dear Heavenly Father,

You understand every feeling and emotion that we experience. You know the deep sadness and loneliness that we feel when there is separation from someone we love. I pray for every reader today, Lord, who is missing someone in their life. Be very near to them and help them to know that You are watching over their loved one. I also pray for every person who is mourning the loss of a person in their life. Comfort them, I pray, Lord, and fill that hole in their heart with Your presence.

In Your name, amen.

"We know that in all things God works for the good of those who love him, who have been called according to his purpose."

ROMANS 8:28

CHAPTER 23
Resisting

As difficult as it had been to part with our special home in Ladner, we had to admit that we really loved Tsawwassen. The unique name of our new community meant "facing the ocean," and our home did exactly that. Every morning felt surreal as I looked out my front patio window and saw the vast Pacific Ocean only a short walk from my front door. The ocean glistened in the sunlight as the seagulls performed a magical dance in flight—just for me, it seemed. I wanted to hold on to this beautiful scene forever, but holding tight to that which I loved had already proven to be futile.

Despite the sale of our Ladner house, the cost of renovations and carrying the debt of two houses took a further toll on our finances. Our paltry incomes couldn't begin to cover our life expenses, let alone tackle our debt. Before we could even begin looking at solutions, Kim got a call from our friend in Kelowna whom we had stayed with during the move. Kelowna was booming, and they needed skilled people in the construction industry. More calls came in. Kim was being headhunted as a project manager and was invited to go there for an interview.

I couldn't even imagine the idea of leaving Tsawwassen and moving again. The mere thought was devastating. We had worked so hard at establishing our lives in Ladner and again in Tsawwassen.

How in the world can we turn our back on what we have accomplished here? We have come so far in our new lives at the coast.

My career was finally moving forward with a unique role in the world of distance education. I had become the test invigilator for students in South Delta who were taking courses with Greater Vancouver Distance Ed. I had also acquired a contract to write a graduation portfolio course for GVDES and oversee the course online. I completed most of this work from my home office in Tsawwassen, with an occasional student or staff meeting in Vancouver.

We were getting more involved in the Tsawwassen Alliance Church and feeling connected to the church community. I often had the chance to sing with the worship team. One woman from the church had become a dear friend, and through her I was developing more quality friendships with women in Tsawwassen.

Kraymer had settled into routines at the hockey academy and his classes at South Delta Senior Secondary. He found a few good friends in the area too and had adjusted well to our move.

The truth was that we had a very good life in Delta despite the financial strains. It would be a huge step backward to leave this place and add more change to our lives.

Kim had no desire to move either, but he realized that something had to change in our world of work and finances. I told Kim to go ahead and talk to the people at the construction company in Kelowna, just so they would quit calling. I refused to go with him. But I did promise to spend time praying about it while he was gone.

So Kim went off to Kelowna for the weekend by himself. I stayed in Tsawwassen. And I kept my promise to pray.

Dear Lord, Your word says that we should not be anxious about anything but should bring everything to You in prayer (Philippians 4:6). Lord, You know exactly what's on my mind today and that the thought of moving again gives me deep anxiety. You also know, Lord, that our finances are in terrible shape and that we have to do something about it. Lord, please guide us, I pray. I don't want to fight over this with Kim, Lord. I pray that we could somehow agree on the best plan for us and our family. Have Your way in our lives, I pray. Amen.

Something completely unexpected happened in me as I prayed.

I had been to Kelowna a few times, and I started to think about the positives of living in a smaller city. Moving and starting all over again was a horrid thought, but my mind kept jumping past that horror to the positives of Kelowna for our family. The more I prayed, the more my heart began to change. I turned to my Bible for confirmation of my thoughts, and a verse from the Psalms nearly leaped off the page— "The righteous will flourish like a palm tree, they will grow like a cedar of Lebanon" (92:12). I felt that God was telling me that our family would flourish in Kelowna.

As soon as Kim got back home and walked in the door, the look on his face told me everything. He had been offered the job in Kelowna and felt that he should take it. He was not looking forward to telling me this, fully expecting another huge fight. My positive reaction to his announcement took him by complete surprise.

As I explained my change of heart, he was affirmed in his decision to accept the job in Kelowna. It was unthinkable to envision what we were committing to. We were actually going to leave our freshly completed oceanside paradise in Tsawwassen and move, again.

YOUR STORY:
Unwanted Change

THINKING BACK
- Have you ever felt like you were at your wits' end with life changes, but then it got even more complicated?
- What was the cause of more unwanted change in your life?

THINKING INWARD
- What strategies of perseverance did you use to cope with the stress of more impending change?
- Did you learn anything about yourself as a person when your tough situation got even tougher?

THINKING OUTWARD
- Were there any options available that would possibly allow you to avoid the greater difficulty? What choices did you have to consider?
- Did you receive any guidance or advice from family or friends as you faced this difficult change?

THINKING FORWARD
- What have you learned from this past challenge that might guide you in the future? What would you say to someone experiencing unwanted change?
- If you are currently facing difficult circumstances in your own life, can you express it to God?

Write a Prayer: Share with God every detail of the unwanted change in your life. Ask for His strength, guidance, and courage to face what comes next.

Dear Heavenly Father,

When You sent Your son Jesus to die on the cross for the sins of all of us, You felt the deep anguish of something "unwanted." Jesus experienced this agony on earth and even prayed, "My Father, if it is possible, may this cup be taken from me. Yet not as I will, but as you will" (Matthew 26:39). Knowing that You understand when we have to face something that we do not want comforts us. I pray for every reader who is in this place today, Lord, and ask that You give them strength and courage to face the unwanted change in their lives. Guide them as they move forward, one step at a time, and help them to persevere.

In Your name, amen.

"When anxiety was great within me,
your consolation brought me joy."

PSALM 94:19

CHAPTER 24

Persevering

I felt a mix of emotions as we descended the mountainous highway into the Okanagan Valley. We had only lived in Tsawwassen for nine months, but we had fallen in love with the oceanside community. An unexplainable opportunity was now drawing us to leave that which we loved and start all over again in the lakeside resort city of Kelowna. It defied logic in many life categories, but it made sense financially. We had both agreed to this move even though we dreaded more change in our lives. We forced ourselves to ignore the knots in our stomach and keep looking forward.

It had only been a few weeks since Kim's first interview in Kelowna, but another trip back to the Okanagan was necessary to finalize our intentions. This time, I went with him, without resistance. We had considered the pros and cons of this new job for him and were choosing to focus on the pros and ignore the cons for now. We needed to discuss the job offer with the owners of the construction company and negotiate details. We also needed to investigate the housing market and begin the search for our next home.

We toured all around Kelowna and considered which area might be the best choice for investing in a house. Getting around Kelowna was so easy compared to navigating the freeways of the lower mainland. The pros of living in a smaller city were already outweighing the cons. I fixed my mind on the good of what lay ahead for us. I could hardly wait to get the packing and moving part over with so we could settle into our lives in this welcoming city.

The company offering Kim a job was one of the builders for a new area in the north end called Wilden. As we explored this corner of Kelowna, we drove past all of the newly constructed homes on the mountainous ridges surrounded by forests. The name "Wilden" came from the word "wilderness"; their slogan was "10 steps to nature, 10 minutes to downtown." The newest subdivision of Wilden being created was an area called Hidden Lake. The unfinished streets were not vehicle ready, but you could walk on them to look at the available lots. One of the perks of working for this company was that Kim would have full access to building his own home. This opportunity appealed to him right from the start.

One of the largest lots in Hidden Lake was lot #32. The far end of the lot jutted out like a peninsula into the little lake. This lot already had a name on it, but right next to it was lot #33, which appeared to claim one corner of the peninsula land. We didn't have much time to make a decision. If we didn't put our name on the lot that weekend, it would soon be taken. We prayed over the piece of land and asked God to guide us—as quickly as possible.

Dear Lord, You have already answered our prayers in so many incredible ways. You have led us to another new place and given us agreement and peace about coming to Kelowna. Lord, You have proven Your guidance in leading us to new homes, and so we come in full confidence of You and ask this again. Help us to know, Lord, if building a house here is the right decision and if buying this piece of land, lot #33, is the best choice or not. Time is of the essence, as You know, Lord, so please help us to make this decision quickly. We ask this in Your name, Lord. Amen.

This time, Kim and I were in full agreement right from the start. We would buy lot #33 and build our first home in Kelowna. We would have to rent for a while as our house was being built, but we could be in the new home by September.

As soon as we got back to Tsawwassen, we put our home on Glenwood Drive up for sale. With all of its renovations and modern interior appeal, there was immediate interest in the house. It only took ten days to finalize a sale. Ironically, we had moved into our Tsawwassen home on April 27, 2005. Exactly one year later, on April 27, 2006, we would be moving out.

Kim committed to starting his new job in March, the first week of spring break. This meant that Kraymer and I could go with him and spend some time in Kelowna during the two weeks of school holidays. I started looking at hotels that would allow us to stay for two weeks, but there were no good options. I found some vacation rentals that might work but could not confirm a place that would also accept our dog, Wally. As usual, I urgently prayed about it, tried not to worry, and hoped that we would find a place when we got there.

When our party of four—two adults, one teenager, and one large furry pooch—arrived in Kelowna, we drove around for a while looking at places we had seen online. Nothing seemed appropriate. We had arranged to meet a rental property manager at a vacation rental condo on Sunset Drive at 4:00 p.m. I didn't feel too hopeful about it since the email said that only small dogs would be allowed. We met her near the front entrance and asked her about our dog, pointing at Wally in the back seat of our truck. She glanced at him and, much to our surprise, said that he was not a problem. He would be accepted.

As we entered the condo unit on the second floor, I was amazed. It was perfect. The two-bedroom fully furnished place came with a fully stocked little kitchen open to a cozy living room. We could stay there for two weeks, and Kim could continue renting after we left. We could even reserve another unit in the same building for May to September while our house was being built. Everything was planned in less than a few minutes. I was blown away by the beauty and speed of these answers to my urgent prayers.

Kim's first weeks on the new job were frustrating. The other project managers were too busy to guide or train him. He had to rely on his self-taught instincts and broad experiences in the construction industry to figure out his role. As he trudged into the condo at the end of a long, hard day, I saw the strain of this new job on him. I could also see the resolve and determination within him to make this work, even though it was not his first choice. He had been enrolled in the "school of hard knocks," but he was determined to persevere and pass every test, one at a time.

Adding to Kim's misery was that sad cloud he didn't talk about, but I knew it was on his mind. Leaving Vancouver meant that he had walked away from his dream of a career in hockey. He remained connected to the team as a scout for the Okanagan area, but his hopes for a career in hockey were fading. Letting go of a dream is never easy, and I prayed that God would give Kim a new sense of purpose in this line of work.

When the two weeks of school holidays were over, our party of four headed back to the lower mainland. But for Kim, it was only a weekend stay. He journeyed back to Kelowna on Sunday evening to tackle his new job early Monday morning. The task ahead of me was not what I wanted to do either; I had to get started on that dreaded packing.

YOUR STORY:

Mixed Emotions

THINKING BACK

- Have you ever accepted a new job or a move to a new city that made sense in your head but not in your heart?
- What caused you to consider this change despite the logic of it?

THINKING INWARD

- Have you ever accepted a new responsibility that felt overwhelming to you? What were your greatest fears about the new role?
- What skills did you have that you could rely on? What strengths, physical or emotional, did you develop at this time?

THINKING OUTWARD

- Have you ever been a student in the "school of hard knocks" when life itself was your teacher? What did you learn? How has that learning influenced the person you are today?
- Were any resources available to you that helped with the challenges that came with this life learning?

THINKING FORWARD

- What have you learned about making decisions with your head when your heart is not in it? How would you guide someone facing this dilemma in the future?
- Are you contemplating any decisions today that make sense on paper but not in your heart?

Write a Prayer: Tell God all about the confusion you are dealing with as you try to figure out a difficult dilemma in your life. Ask for His wisdom to guide your thoughts about this decision.

Dear Heavenly Father,

Life presents us with many decisions and dilemmas that are difficult and confusing. I pray for readers today, Lord, who are in this uncomfortable place, and I ask that You draw near to them and comfort them. You, O God, are the one who can change our hearts, so I ask that You help all those whose hearts are not dedicated to the task they face. Help them to find the strength, courage, and stamina to accomplish what needs to be done.

In Your name, amen.

"The LORD is near to all who call on him,
to all who call on him in truth."

PSALM 145:18

CHAPTER 25
Amazed

I sealed another box and carelessly scribbled a label. I kicked it into the corner as if it was filled with useless junk. My attitude had picked up a whole lot of "battitude" during the process of boxing up our belongings again. All of my initial faith and optimism about this move to Kelowna were nowhere to be found. I despised every empty box and loathed the work ahead of me.

There is nothing in this world I hate more than packing! Why did I agree to this plan of moving again?

My body was not physically suffering from the packing as it had in previous moves, but I was struggling emotionally. Saying goodbye to our lives in the lower mainland was even more difficult than I had expected. It had been challenging to adjust from life on the farm to the city lifestyle, but we had conquered it. Our family had faced the task of surviving a 180-degree life change, and we had pulled it off. We had learned how to navigate freeways, endure traffic jams, and handle the pace of life in Greater Vancouver. We had adjusted to a whole new culture. It seemed like we were walking away from a successful transition.

Life in Kelowna would be totally different. We had to find a new home, new jobs, new church, and new friends.

Why do we have to start over and rebuild our lives from the bottom … again? Finding work that I enjoy was so challenging in Delta; how will I ever find a job in Kelowna?

Even though I didn't feel like it, I committed this new start to God in prayer, asking Him to bless all aspects of our next new beginning. I had to remind myself of the promise that I felt God had given me a few months earlier and retain the belief that our family would "flourish" in Kelowna.

Dear Lord, I praise You for all that You are. You are our creator, our saviour, and our shepherd. You know me as the shepherd knows his sheep, Lord, and You know exactly how I am feeling today. I am trying to recall the peace and the energy that I had when we decided to go ahead with this move. It seemed like You gave us clear direction about moving to Kelowna, even though I'm just not feeling it today. Your Spirit was so clearly present when You spoke to me through Psalm 92. But today, that awesome promise seems lost to me. You have already guided us in so many ways, Lord; please help me to trust You again and to draw the strength from You that I need to get this move done.

One more thing, Lord. I've been too busy packing to plan what I will do for work in Kelowna. But the nagging dread of looking for another job is one of the dark clouds over my head. So, I am going to commit that huge need to You, too. Thank You, Lord. Amen.

A moving truck pulling up in front of our house was an all too familiar sight. This time, however, the load was much smaller. Kim had already hauled a lot of our stuff during his weekend trips.

As the moving truck was fully loaded and heading off to the Okanagan, it felt like déjà vu of the day we left Saskatchewan. I followed behind the truck a few hours later, with all the last-minute stuff jammed into my SUV. It seemed like the engine of my loaded down Santa Fe felt exactly the same as my dragging spirits. It laboured wearily up the Coquihalla Highway.

As we reached the toll at the peak of the Coquihalla Highway, we seemed to pick up speed. The trip got noticeably easier. I felt my energy shift and my spirits rise as we neared Kelowna. The hardest part was behind us.

We can do this. It's going to get better. Unpacking is easier than packing.

We were closer now to the positive place I had envisioned a few months before. The next phase of our lives would soon begin, even though it held many unknowns. We had a temporary home waiting for us on Sunset Drive, so at least we knew where we were going as we entered the city.

I was allowed to teach one last online course for GVDES that summer but would not be able to continue working for GVDES when I lived outside of the lower mainland. I had to let that go too. I didn't know where else to look for work in our new city, so I submitted my resumé to School District 23. I had heard about this school district and their innovative career planning programs when we were still living in Saskatchewan. I assumed I would have to go back to the dreaded world of TOC work to get my foot in the door with SD 23.

My resumé drew unexpected attention. The BC Ministry of Education had recently mandated that all grade twelve students must have a completed graduation portfolio before graduating. Administrative staffs from schools were scrambling to find teachers who could help implement this new mandate. My knowledge of portfolios was a desired commodity.

To my shock and delight, the human resource director with SD 23 contacted me about two positions that might be available to me.

My first interview was at Mount Boucherie Senior Secondary School. I was interested but not convinced that it was the right place for me. My second interview took place at George Elliot Secondary School in Lake Country. For some reason, I felt comfortable in that school as soon as I entered the door. The interview went much better than the one at Mount Boucherie, and I accepted the job at George Elliot.

I marvelled all summer at how God had opened the doors for me to work in Kelowna. Typically, it would have taken years on the TOC list to get a position with SD 23, and here I was with a full-time one-year contract. My main duty would not be teaching; I would be the career program and portfolio coordinator.

My mind drifted back to the vision I had experienced in Saskatchewan. God told me there would be change coming to our lives. He also told me to pay attention to portfolios. They would be important in my future. That was seven years before. How amazing! I didn't realize at the time how or when the vision would come to pass.

YOUR STORY:

New Beginnings

THINKING BACK

- Have you ever lived through a change in your life that allowed you to have a blessed new beginning? What aspects of this blessing surprised you the most?
- As you think back, can you recall any hints, premonitions, or guidance about the nature of this blessing?

THINKING INWARD

- Sometimes life seems most dark and difficult "just before dawn" or just before a blessing arrives in your life. Have you ever had this experience?
- How did you cope with this dark time? What gave you hope or encouragement to keep forging ahead?

THINKING OUTWARD

- How did this new beginning line up with other aspects of your life circumstances?
- Were any other people involved in this blessing? Did they experience benefits from your blessing?

THINKING FORWARD

- What have you learned from your experiences of new beginnings that might guide you in the future?
- Are you still in a place of desire, waiting, or hoping, for a new beginning?

Write a Prayer: Tell God every aspect of a new beginning that you desire. Commit the details to Him and trust that His plan for your life will prevail.

Dear Heavenly Father,

You always go before us and prepare a way for us that we do not even know about. You are the creator of new beginnings. In Isaiah 43:18–19, You said, "Forget the former things; do not dwell on the past. See, I am doing a new thing! Now it springs up; do you not perceive it?" Lord, I pray for all readers who are experiencing a new beginning today. Open their minds to perceive what You are doing in their lives. Help them to let go of people or places from their former lives they might be clinging to and not dwell on things from their past. May they recognize the gifts in the new things You are leading them to. Thank You, Lord, for the way You make new things "spring up" for us.

In Your name, amen.

"For the revelation awaits an appointed time;
it speaks of the end and will not prove false.
Though it linger, wait for it;
it will certainly come and will not delay."

HABAKKUK 2:3

CHAPTER 26
Unsettled

Hot summer weather with lots of sunshine, a condo with two swimming pools, smooth sandy beaches just a short walk away: these were the postcard images we hoped to experience our first summer of living in Kelowna. Our temporary home, a condo on the lake in our new resort city, promised us a summer to remember. It was, indeed, unforgettable.

Before the boys and I arrived in April, Kim had already moved to the fifth floor of the condo building on Sunset Drive. It was a bigger unit at the far end that had amazing views of Okanagan Lake. We could see the vehicles crossing the William Bennett Bridge and the pockets of homes on the west side of the lake. Below us was a beach that led to the boardwalk along the lake and the Delta Hotel. Kim's new fitness routine included a scenic run along the boardwalk, and I relished my long lakeside walks with Wally down to City Park. We were all looking forward to the hot weather so we could take advantage of the two outdoor swimming pools in the condominium complex.

Just as the warmer weather arrived, we received a notice under our door. When we had arrived in March, the underground parking was blocked off, and we were not allowed to use it since repair work was being done. It turned out that the cracks in the walls of the underground parking area led to a harsh discovery. The building had not been built to code. It was lacking major weight-bearing beams. The letter under our door announced that our condo building was officially declared "UNSAFE." All residents were advised to move out as soon as possible.

Residents of the condo building received the news with different perspectives. Some began to pack immediately and moved out as soon as they could find a place to go to. Others scoffed at the news and felt no sense of urgency to get out. We were somewhere in between the two groups. We only needed to live there a few more months, and then our house being built on Hidden Lake Place in Wilden would be ready for us. Finding and moving to yet another rental property was the last thing we wanted to do. We decided to stick it out.

Much to our extreme disappointment, the pools and fitness room were no longer available to residents. Pools and hot tubs were drained, turning into large dusty holes. The fitness room was locked up. Underground parking was already forbidden, but now it was boarded up with huge signs blocking the entry. Everyone who continued to live there had to fight for the limited amount of street parking available. We got a small deduction in our rent for the loss of amenities, but it didn't ease our disappointment or buy us any peace of mind.

Kim's state of mind was not only lacking peace, he was on overload. He had been assigned the task of managing the construction of a condominium building outside of Kelowna on the mountain of Big White. The five-storey building was located right next to the gondola for the ski hill. This huge task had extra challenges since there was no one near the site to help him solve problems when questions or issues came up. He simply had to figure it out himself. It was another course in the "school of hard knocks," with a very steep learning curve. I prayed for him every morning, as I could see that this work was far from easy. The pay for this job was better than any pay he had received in the lower mainland, but the stress level was also much greater.

Dear Lord, please be very near to my husband. He has chosen to take on this new job even though it is not really the desire of his heart. It is taking him farther away from his goals and dreams. Help him, I pray, to get guidance for this job and to find some type of satisfaction in this work. Thank You, Lord, that You never leave us or forsake us. Amen.

Kraymer went off with his dad to Big White most days during the summer to help out with general cleanup on the construction site. Kolby found a summer job with the same construction company as well, in general labour and construction at Sonoma Pines on the west side.

Getting enough groceries up to the fifth floor of our condo to feed my hungry crew of hardworking guys was a challenge. I came up with the idea of using a very large suitcase with wheels. I kept the suitcase in the back of my SUV and put the bags of groceries directly into the suitcase. I could just wheel the suitcase up to the front door of the condo, then take the elevator to the fifth floor. I wondered if the neighbours were curious as to why I "moved in" and "moved out" several times a week with my large suitcase.

Not only did our first summer in Kelowna bring disheartening news and bitter disappointment, the fall brought added frustrations. Our Hidden Lake house was supposed to be ready in September, but it was delayed till November. Our warmer clothes and winter jackets were packed up somewhere in the towers of boxes at the back of our storage units. We would have to go digging for them.

As the days grew colder and signs of summer disappeared, there were fewer tenants but still many of us living in the "unsafe" condo building. Adding to our list of unsettling setbacks, another notice arrived under our door with more confusing news. The note indicated that our dog was far beyond the acceptable size of dogs for this condo and would no longer be allowed to live there.

Wally had already lived there with us for many months. Obviously, someone had complained. We could not imagine sending Wally off to live somewhere else. He was part of our family.

If we can just hold on for two more months, our family, including Wally, will be okay.

I scheduled an appointment with the building manager and prayed that he would be sympathetic to our situation. When we met to discuss the letter, I informed him that we had originally been told that Wally was accepted to live there when we first moved in. I pleaded with him to let Wally stay since we would all be moving out as soon as possible. To my relief, he agreed that Wally could stay, under one condition. At the building manager's request, we started using the back stairwell to take him out during the day, and we avoided the elevator whenever he was with us. As long as the remaining tenants did not submit further complaints, we could push Wally's permit to stay with us until we all moved out. We got extra exercise the next two months, going up and down five flights of stairs with Wally several times a day.

Despite the disappointments of living in Kelowna that first summer, I clung to the excitement of starting my new position at George Elliot School. Adjusting to full-time work in a school, however, was more difficult than I expected. I had so much to learn about how things worked at this secondary school in Lake Country.

The teacher who had previously done some of the work that was now my responsibility had passed away suddenly the year before, so there was no direct transfer of knowledge or program information available to me. The staff at George Elliot, however, was welcoming, considerate, and helpful; I appreciated every teacher and staff member who patiently helped me get oriented to my new job.

Adding to the busyness of the first few months of teaching, I often had to rush to building supply stores after school. Kim was still working in Big White, so I needed to confirm our kitchen cabinet details, flooring choices, and many other decisions for the new house. The last thing we wanted was to hold up the possession date of our new home due to choices not made in time for the trades to complete the finishing work.

Kraymer was starting school at Kelowna Senior Secondary, so he had another huge adjustment to make as well. Fortunately, our son who didn't used to like change had become quite used to it. He faced starting grade eleven at a new school with bravery beyond his years. His only comment at the end of the first day was that schools are basically the same; teachers and classes are no different from one school to the next.

Kolby's first priority of the fall was to find a team where he could continue playing his best level of hockey. He decided to try out for the Westside Warriors and was successful in making the team. We hadn't expected both boys to be living with us that fall, and the two-bedroom condo was rather small for the four of us, especially with added clothes for colder weather and hockey equipment. The boys shared an extremely small bedroom with one tiny closet. This was far from ideal living conditions for our two large athletic guys. My heart ached for them and the lack of privacy they had to endure.

We all longed for the completion of our new home in November.

YOUR STORY:

Life Setbacks

THINKING BACK

- Can you recall a time in your life when everything seemed to be moving forward, but then a setback made life much more challenging?
- What events caused this setback? Was there any way to avoid it?

THINKING INWARD

- As you recall the disappointments that you had to endure, what was your belief about what was happening in your life at the time?
- How did you cope emotionally with the details of the setback?

THINKING OUTWARD

- Did anyone support you or help you manage the setback season? Did you receive guidance or wise advice from anyone who had experienced this in their lives?
- How long did you have to endure the setback before you felt you could move forward with life again? What life event(s) or attitude shifts allowed you to push forward?

THINKING FORWARD

- What have you learned about yourself or life in general through this setback? Is there any aspect of this life experience that will guide you in the future?
- Are you or your loved ones living in a "setback season" today? What are your hopes and prayers for surviving this disappointing time?

Write a Prayer: Tell God the frustrating details of this season of your life. Ask Him to replace discouragement and doubt with renewed hope and optimism.

Dear Heavenly Father,

Many of us have had experiences in life when we were following a path we believed to be Your plan for our lives. Everything was falling into place until a series of troubling situations occurred. It is hard to understand these setbacks. I pray for every reader, Lord, who is experiencing a season of troubling times. I ask that You would guide them through each setback they encounter. Help them to find a way of dealing with each challenge as it arrives, one at a time, until the season ends. Thank You, Lord, that these seasons are temporary.

In Your name, amen.

"For our light and momentary troubles are achieving for us an eternal glory that far outweighs them all. So we fix our eyes not on what is seen, but what is unseen, since what is seen is temporary, but what is unseen is eternal."

2 CORINTHIANS 4:17–18

CHAPTER 27
Blessed

Moving to the just-completed new house on Hidden Lake Place was like a fantasy coming to reality. Not only did we have our own front door with no elevator or stairs to climb, we had space beyond belief.

Our craftsman-style home had a large two-car garage that led into a spacious mudroom right next to a massive kitchen with a big pantry. We had over 3,600 square feet, with two spare bedrooms upstairs and a large master bedroom with a full-sized ensuite and walk-in closet on the main level. The lower level had two more bedrooms, another family room, and a full-sized fitness room. The boys now had their very own big bedrooms with large closets and a spacious bathroom all to themselves. It actually felt a bit lonely the first few days. It was hard to find each other in that big house.

Having a home with a permanent address again meant everything to me. It was more valuable and appreciated this time than any previous address. We were no longer visitors in Kelowna but settled residents. We already had jobs, schools, hockey teams, and a few neighbours. We belonged in this city.

After moving to the new house in November, my commute to work was much shorter. I was starting to feel connections with the school staff, developing some quality friendships with a few of the people who worked closely with me. I was also a member of the district team creating our own unique guidelines for the graduation portfolio requirement of SD 23.

Kim was still leaving early in the morning, determined to be the first to arrive at his building site at Big White. He was solving one problem at a time, and the condominium project was slowly reaching completion. He took pride in the details of each unit as the ski chalet decor came alive with finishing touches.

Our first Christmas at Hidden Lake Place was a truly joyful occasion. Our stone fireplace with matching stone archway leading into the great room was the perfect background for decorative greenery and stockings. Our out-of-the-ordinary wood doors and baseboards mimicked the look of the ski chalets at Big White, providing a cozy "winter getaway" atmosphere. Our little corner of land on the peninsula that jutted out to Hidden Lake had become a special fire pit area, an inviting spot to all friends and relatives who came to visit. We were pleased to have our nephew and his wife, who had recently moved to BC, join us for our first Christmas in Kelowna.

As the colder temperatures arrived in December, Hidden Lake became a massive outdoor skating rink that the whole neighbourhood enjoyed. When the snow fell, the skating enthusiasts were out on the ice shovelling and scraping clean some mini hockey rinks for local kids to practice their game. It brought back familiar cherished memories for this family from Saskatchewan who had learned to skate on the dugout next to our farm.

Wally and I took long walks on the paths around the lake and into the forested areas surrounding our home. The scenery was completely different than our walks to the ocean at Tsawwassen but captivating in its own way. I have always been a lover of trees, and the forests of Wilden lured me to explore them further. The aroma of the pine trees was distinctive, and I soon learned, after a bit of research, that there were health benefits to this quality time in the forest.

I found a special tree not far from our house that I named my prayer tree since I often paused there to talk to God. It was the perfect place to stop and pray about whatever was on my heart and to express my appreciation for all that God had provided.

Dear Lord, my heart is overflowing with gratitude for all the different environments that we have been blessed to experience in the last few years. You have led us to many new places and brought us to many new experiences. You have been with us through the good and the bad and helped us with each difficulty, one at a time. Our new home in Kelowna is the greatest blessing yet, Lord, and I cannot thank You enough for every detail of it and this lovely pocket of the world known as Wilden that we now get to call home. Thanks be unto You, dear Lord, for Your never-ending love and for every good gift that You give to Your children. Amen.

As 2006 came to a close, I could not help but sigh and pray more prayers of deep gratitude, expressing contentment with our new life in Kelowna. Kim had made great progress with his job. My position at George Elliot Secondary was going well. Kolby was back home with us, and Kraymer had adjusted to yet another new school. Even Wally had settled into this new home, even though it was the fourth place he had lived in the four years of his life so far.

YOUR STORY:

Times of Contentment

THINKING BACK

- Can you recall a time in your life when you felt very blessed? What led you to this place of contentment?
- What hardships did you have to endure before your season of contentment?

THINKING INWARD

- What were the "sweet spots" of this place of contentment? Why did they mean so much to you?
- What did you learn about yourself during this season of contentment?

THINKING OUTWARD

- How were your family or friends affected by your blessings? Were you able to bless others through the good fortune you experienced?
- Have you found a way to celebrate or honour your blessings and express your deepest feelings of gratitude?

THINKING FORWARD

- What have you learned about the importance of gratitude that you will practice in the future?
- How can you express your gratitude to God for who He is and for every good thing He has done for you?

Write a Prayer: Create a list for God of every detail in your life that you are thankful for. Keep the list handy so that you can add to it daily and continue the habit of gratitude.

Dear Heavenly Father,

We so often come to You and repeatedly ask, ask, and ask for help, guidance, healing, and blessings. Today, dear Lord, we simply want to thank You and give glory to Your name. You told us how important this is through the story of the ten lepers in Luke 17. You healed ten of them, yet only one returned to give You glory. We do not want to be like the nine who simply left to enjoy their blessings. We want to pause and acknowledge You as the true giver of all good gifts. We worship, honour, and thank You, Lord.

In Your matchless and holy name, amen.

"Now to the King eternal, immortal, invisible, the only God, be honor and glory for ever and ever. Amen."

1 TIMOTHY 1:17

CHAPTER 28
Emptied

You know it's coming. You try not to think about it, but denial does not make it go away. Eventually your children will leave the nest and begin to plan their own lives. For us, it seemed extra bittersweet, since we were barely settled in Kelowna when it started. We were just becoming rooted in our new city, and it seemed that our family would indeed "flourish" in this place.

I have learned, however, that our limited perspective cannot comprehend God's timing and His perfect plan. He sees and knows the bigger picture and has the blueprint perfectly designed for our lives. What we see and experience in the present often doesn't make any sense until later. Instead of 2007 bringing stability to our family life, it brought more unexpected changes.

Kolby was traded from the Westside Warriors to Powell River. This was not where he wanted to go, so he decided to return to Briercrest College in Saskatchewan, where he could play college-level hockey again and continue working on a business degree. He had less than two months to enjoy his big new bedroom with a view of Hidden Lake before heading back to a dorm room in Caronport, Saskatchewan.

Shortly after saying goodbye to his big brother, Kraymer was called up to play with the Vancouver Giants. This meant he would have to go back to Vancouver and temporarily live with billets. Saying goodbye to one son was hard enough. Watching both boys leave the home we had just nicely settled into was like a bad dream. The absence of both boys was only for a few months, but it seemed like the worst possible timing.

It was just the two of us now, with Wally, of course, living in this big 3,600 square foot house. We tried to bask in the luxury of this space and enjoy a couch of our own to stretch out on in the evenings, but it was not at all satisfying. It was our first phase of being empty nesters, and it was, indeed, empty.

If there was one positive to this new phase of life, it was that both Kim and I had demanding work lives to consume our minds. Kim was still dealing with the ongoing challenges of finishing the condominium building at Big White. I was taking on new challenges at George Elliot Secondary School in Winfield. Additional courses had been added to my teaching position for the second semester, on top of implementing our new version of the graduation portfolio and planning a portfolio presentation event for all of our GE grads.

Fortunately, the first phase of our empty nest didn't last long, and both boys were back under our roof before summer. But something else happened that summer that signalled the next major change that would shift the dynamics of our family.

Kolby was invited to be one of the groomsmen in the wedding party of a good friend he had met at Briercrest. The wedding was to take place in Alberta, so off he went, fully prepared with his handsome groomsman attire. When he returned home, we noticed a new twinkle in his eye and an extra hop in his step. He spent hours on the phone every evening. It took a few days, but he finally let us in on the most exciting part of the wedding for him. He had met someone—someone special. She was the bridesmaid he had been randomly partnered with for walking down the aisle.

We could see that Kolby was totally smitten with this new friend in his life and that he felt the relationship had potential. I had prayed many times for the future wives of my sons, but this new development in Kolby's life was a clear sign that I needed to take those prayers to a new level.

Dear Lord, I am amazed all over again at how You work in our lives and how You lead us to places and people that You want us to meet. Lord, I thank You for this young woman Kolby has met and for the spark of hope and excitement that it has given him. I pray for Your total guidance and protection on both of their lives as they get to know each other via distance. I pray they would know if they are well-suited for each other, Lord, and that their relationship would grow according to Your perfect plan for their lives. I place both of them in Your hands, Lord, and am just so grateful that You have all this figured out already. In Your precious name, Lord. Amen.

The fall brought phase two of our empty-nester world with Kraymer returning to Vancouver and Kolby heading back to Saskatchewan again. The quiet, empty house was a bit easier to handle the second time, but we both knew that this phase would be longer, with a more unpredictable ending. The reality was that our boys were growing into young men. We were very proud of who they were becoming but would have given anything to hold on to them just a little longer.

YOUR STORY:

Changes to Family

THINKING BACK

- What were the first signs that signalled the arrival of a change in your family situation? How did you react to these signs?
- What circumstances or other factors in your life made the impending change a challenging time for you?

THINKING INWARD

- What emotions did you experience as you dealt with the changing dynamics of your family?
- How did you fill the additional time and space that you had in your life? Were there any blessings in it for you?

THINKING OUTWARD

- Did you seek advice or comfort from others who had experienced similar changes?
- Sometimes changes in our families happen in phases and requires adjusting back and forth from empty house to full again. If you experienced this, what challenges have you encountered as you moved from one phase to another and back again?

THINKING FORWARD

- If change to your family dynamic is still in your future, do you feel you will be ready for it? Is there something you can do to prepare yourself for this change?
- Have you prayed or are you currently praying over the future partners of your children?

Write a Prayer: Commit your family of the future to God. Give Him every worry and concern that you have. Trust Him to be in the midst of every detail.

Dear Heavenly Father,

You have shown us repeatedly that Your ways are so much higher than our ways. Even though changes and situations in our lives do not make sense to us, You are in control and You know the end of the story. I pray for every reader who is experiencing a change in their family situation. Be very near to them today and comfort their concerns and their loneliness. Guide them to new people and places that will help fill their empty hearts. Help us as parents to keep trusting You regarding the choices of our adult children. And help us, I pray, to leave our every worry and concern with You.

In Your name, amen.

"Trust in him at all times, you people;
pour out your hearts to him,
for God is our refuge."

PSALM 62:8

CHAPTER 29
Still Learning

Not only was the house quiet and lonely when both boys left for a second time in September, this time it felt extra empty. My sadness doubled since I no longer had a job to consume my mind and my time.

What do you have planned for me now, Lord? Is this the time to become a student again?

The goal and desire to complete a master's degree had been planted in my mind while we were still living in Saskatchewan. I had started with a few classes through Athabasca University but quit the program due to my mom's cancer diagnosis. I was about to start again while we lived in Tsawwassen but had to pull my name from the Delta cohort of UBC when our move to Kelowna was confirmed. Since I had a fully accepted application for the master's in education program at UBC in Vancouver, I was able to transfer this acceptance to UBC Okanagan.

In the fall of 2008, despite fear of a third cancellation and a lack of confidence in my learning abilities at this age, I enrolled in the new master's of education program in Kelowna. Entering the classroom as a student instead of a teacher felt odd and exhilarating at the same time. As I looked around at my classmates, I spotted a few in my age category, but most were much younger.

What am I doing? I am nearing the age of 50. Do I still have the ability to study and write papers like I could 30 years ago?

My third start with MEd studies turned out to be the triumphant one and most perfectly suited to my circumstances. I now lived an easy ten-minute drive from the newly developed UBC Okanagan campus. Courses for this new master's program took place on weekends and during the summer, so I could still accept other work and keep earning an income. The program focused on teaching and learning and allowed us to complete projects and research on areas of our chosen interest in education. I decided to focus on adult learners and research how adults can prove and possibly deepen their learning for the purpose of a portfolio.

I loved the challenge that every course proposed and consumed my mind with every short research paper that I had the chance to write. But I struggled to come up with the framework needed to develop the research focus for my thesis. By the first summer of our studies, most of my classmates were well into their thesis development. I still didn't have a plan laid out for mine, and the pressure of the decision was weighing heavily on my mind. I had considered several different directions for my thesis, but as I read, studied, and prepared notes on each one, I just didn't have peace about any of them. I prayed desperately for God to give me a creative idea that would provide a useful framework.

Dear Lord, You know how thankful I am to finally be making progress on this master's degree. You are the one who opened the door for me to get into this program and chose the most perfect place and time for me to finally be able to do this. Now, dear Lord, I need Your divine guidance as to how to do my thesis. Please give me some direction, I pray, as I want this work to be useful to You, Lord. I ask this in Your name, Lord. Amen.

A new idea came to me a month later, and I felt it was the answer to my prayer. Researching and developing this idea gave me energy and peace. The concept of reflecting about past learning in a purposeful way using four different perspectives became my framework. I named the four perspectives and chose the title "The Four Dimensions of Reflection" for my thesis. Literature I reviewed on the topic confirmed that when we purposefully reflect on previous learning, using criteria with meaningful questions, we can recall that learning with added perspective and possibly deepen the learning.

"The Four Dimensions of Reflection," as described in the prologue, has since been published in a Ministry of Education book named *Innovations in Education* and also in a book called *A Teaching Artist's Companion* by an educator in New York, Daniel Levy. It has been downloaded hundreds of times from my blog and used by teachers and professors of many types of courses.

The day I picked up my certificate for my MEd degree at UBC Okanagan, I was offered work as a faculty advisor, observing student teachers who were completing their practicum with School District #23. For the next four years, I spent time in many different schools in Kelowna, observing and evaluating new teachers' abilities to teach French and other subjects. In 2011, I was offered a contract at Okanagan College to be one of the instructors in the certificate program called "Learner Centred Instruction." A key component of these courses is reflection—using a reflective lens to develop and monitor teaching effectiveness.

I am so grateful for the opportunity to continue my formal learning. I can see God's leading in all of the choices—the where, when, and how of my learning pursuits. The beauty of our lives designed by God is that we never stop learning and evolving. Our purpose continues—regardless of our location, life situation, or age.

YOUR STORY:
A Time of Peak Learning

THINKING BACK
- Can you identify a time in your life when you experienced significant learning about a subject area or about life?
- Where were you and how did this time of learning begin for you?

THINKING INWARD
- Can you recall an "aha moment" when full understanding of what you were trying to learn took place?
- What emotions did you experience as you realized your newly acquired learning?

THINKING OUTWARD
- Who played the greatest role in leading you to this learning? Did a parent, a friend, a teacher, or a professor influence your attitude to learning?
- How did family or friends react to your new levels of learning?

THINKING FORWARD
- How will this learning experience influence learning choices of the future?
- What area of learning do you desire for your future?

Write a Prayer: Express your gratitude to God, thanking Him for the learning He has led you to experience in your life. Ask Him to guide you to the next time and place where you will be able to learn and gain knowledge and more understanding of life.

Dear Heavenly Father,

I lift up to You every person who picks up this book and reads even a portion of the content. I pray, dear Lord, that You will use my humble stories and prayers to speak to the readers' hearts. May You draw them closer to You and help them to realize how You have already been working in their lives and how You desire to have a closer relationship with them. May Your purpose for their lives become clearer, and may they move into their future with more faith, more hope, and more confidence in Your divine guidance.

In Your name, amen.

"The prayer of a righteous person is powerful and effective."

JAMES 5:16

If any of my stories or the guided reflections have impacted you, I would love to hear from you. Please send any comments or questions about ideas expressed in the book to kybarnstable@gmail.com.

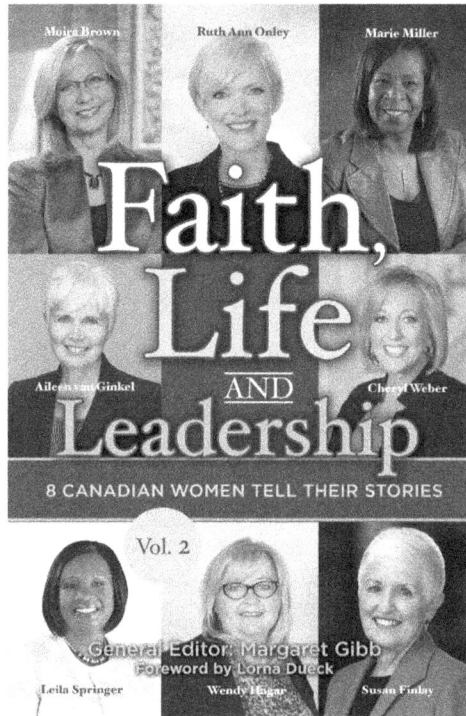

"Each one of these unique, personal, and vulnerable stories points to a bigger story: God's powerful story of calling, redemption, faithfulness, healing, provision, protection, and impact. You can't help being encouraged."
—**Dr. Steve Brown**, president of Arrow Leadership, author of *Leading Me*

"What makes this book compelling reading is to see and marvel at how God can take the raw materials of our lives—strengths, weaknesses, accomplishments, and failings—and fashion something beautiful and fruitful beyond our imagining."
—**Janet Clark**, PhD, senior VP Academic, Tyndale University College and Seminary

"As you discover these women, you will discover too how God has been working with your life for the good works prepared for you. Settle in for a good curious journey with the remarkable women in these pages."
—**Lorna Dueck**, CEO of Crossroads Christian Communications and YES TV

CASTLE QUAY BOOKS

RISEN FROM PRISON

BEYOND MY WILDEST IMAGINATION

BOSCO H.C. POON

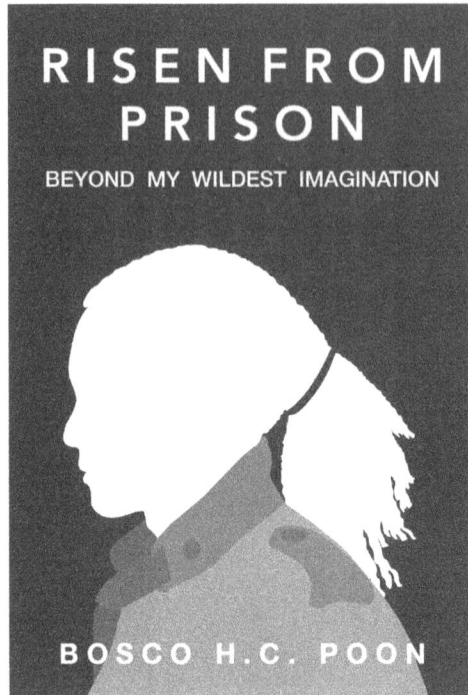

Risen From Prison is B.O.Z's autobiography and chronicles his early life as an immigrant to Canada; the challenges he faced in his journey from musical success to gang involvement, arrest, trial, and incarceration; his spiritual redemption; and the many miracles that occurred after his decision to follow Jesus Christ. From the top of the world to the pits of prison life and back out by the hand of God, B.O.Z calls everything that happened in his life "beyond his wildest imagination." B.O.Z recounts this fascinating story with openness and vulnerability in the hope that others who have separated from God may find their way to Him also.

"Boz's story is gripping. What starts out tragically ends with layers of beautiful redemption. I remember our first meeting. It was in the prison in Mission, BC, where I would occasionally sing for the inmates—he wanted to talk up his music business connections. I liked Boz right away and I knew that our meeting wasn't about the music business; I could sense God's call on his life. It was only a matter of time until he surrendered himself to Jesus's voice of love speaking to him. His life and this book are powerful reminders of what God can do with any of us who surrender our will and choose to serve and live God's way wherever we are."

—**Brian Doerksen**, Christian singer-songwriter

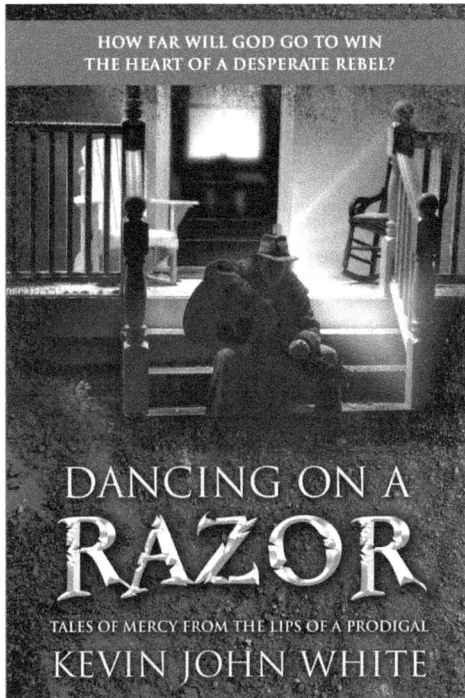

HOW FAR WILL GOD GO TO WIN
THE HEART OF A DESPERATE REBEL?

DANCING ON A
RAZOR
TALES OF MERCY FROM THE LIPS OF A PRODIGAL
KEVIN JOHN WHITE

"I was as moved by Kevin's devastating and glorious story as I was by his manner of telling it ... *Dancing on a Razor* is humbling and beautiful."
—**Steve Bell**, singer-songwriter, author

"This is a remarkable book! ... Kevin reveals how he was in the battle zone between Heaven and Hell and what it is really like to enter into the pit of hopelessness. Yet God never forgets about him."
—**Rev. Dr. Alistair P. Petrie**, executive director of Partnership Ministries

"Kevin White walks readers through the dark worlds he's known, ultimately to find the most radiant of lights awaiting at the end of each one."
—**Tim Huff**, author, speaker, social-justice worker

CASTLE QUAY BOOKS

BECAUSE GOD WAS THERE

A JOURNEY OF LOSS, HEALING AND OVERCOMING

BELMA VARDY

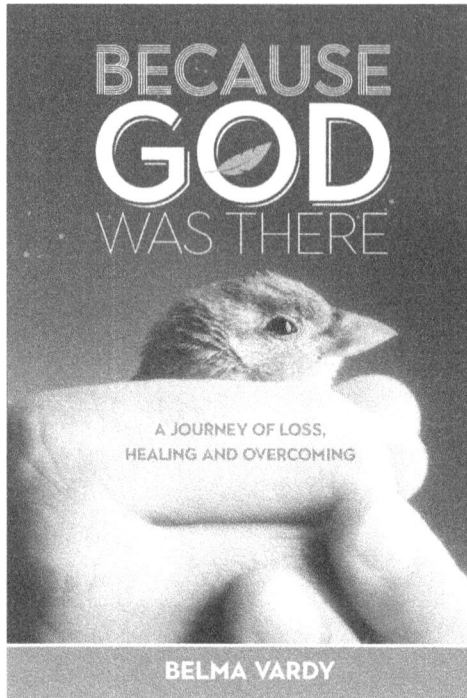

"Get this book not only for yourself, but buy copies for your friends. It may just save their life. This is real!"—**Barbara Yoder**, apostle, Shekinah, Ann Arbor, MI

"*Because God Was There* will take you deep into the spiritual realm. This book should be in every counsellor's office."—**Moira Brown**, TV and radio personality

"What a story! This book should be turned into a movie."
—**Steve and Sandra Long**, senior leaders, Catch the Fire, Toronto

"A manual to lead you from tragedy to triumph."
—**Barry Maracle** (Mohawk), Desert Stream Ministries

"A must-read for every person who has ever experienced trauma or hurts in life, especially Indian residential/boarding school survivors."
—**Dr. Gerard and Peta-Gay Roberts**

"This down-to-earth book will bring hope, encouragement and fresh vision."
—**Mary Audrey Raycroft**, international speaker

CASTLE QUAY BOOKS

www.ingramcontent.com/pod-product-compliance
Lightning Source LLC
Chambersburg PA
CBHW032058080426
42733CB00006B/330